Brief Lives:
The Art of the Obituary

by Chuck Anderson

PublishAmerica
Baltimore

First printing

PublishAmerica has allowed this work to remain exactly as the author intended, verbatim, without editorial input.

Softcover 9781627724425
PUBLISHED BY PUBLISHAMERICA, LLLP
www.publishamerica.com
Baltimore

Printed in the United States of America

obituary : noun, from obituarius, medieval Latin, an announcement, especially in a newspaper, of someone's death, often with a short biography.

For almost 25 years, the author worked as a reporter and occasional editor for the Long Island Advance, a newspaper published on Long Island, New York. After writing one or two obituaries, he was often asked by local families to memorialize a departed relative. He learned that the secret to writing an obituary was not to talk about how the person died, but, rather, how he or she lived, and what they contributed to the community. For example, many of the obituaries in this collection reflect that the subjects were members of the "greatest generation," Americans who went overseas to defend freedom during World War II.

This is their story.

Table of Contents

A Sailor's Final Voyage:
Robert Westaway Starke

Brookhaven Hamlet, a small community on the South Shore of Long Island, is an unlikely place for nobility, but if there were a royal family, its patriarch would have been Robert Westaway Starke, who died at the age of 90 on June 6. At his bedside in their home on Bay Road was his wife Helen, who would have shared their 65th wedding anniversary the next day.

Growing up in the house his father built in the 1900s, Bob Starke attended the Brookhaven Elementary School just up the street. He went on to Erasmus High School, cultivating what was to become a lifetime love affair with reading, especially mysteries and the classics. Later in life, when he and his son David, who became an executive with 20th Century Fox, were looking at colleges, he had to "inspect every library." Every night, he would read to his children before they went to bed. Even in his 80s, with failing eyesight, he could be found rereading Homer with a magnifying glass.

An avid sailor, he won the Queen of the Bay Race a number of times in the sloop Elvira and other boats.

He was also an accomplished rider, keeping a horse in the city and bringing it out to the country in the summers. He and Betty Wellington Puleston staged a horse show in the '30s, a percursor to the Hamptons Classic.

He attended Dartmouth for a year, then answered the call of the sea, sailing as a cadet on the Robin Line, delivering mail to such places as Zanzibar and Mozambique. His son John, a film producer, said, "He spoke to us in nautical terms all our lives, referring to us as 'scrubs'"

While in Johannesburg, Africa, Starke met the British representatives of a company that needed plastic parts. Back in the states, he arranged for a ship to take parts to the company, but the Germans sank it. On June 7, 1941, he married Helen, and they went back to Africa with another shipload of parts.

They stayed in South Africa for two years. Returning to the U.S., Bob Starke joined the Navy, and due to his background in plastics, was assigned to the Naval Ordinance Laboratory at Silver Springs, MD. During his free time, he designed a small sailing dinghy, which would become popular in the Fireplace Frostbite races held on the Carmans River in the winter months. When sailors capsized in those races, they would be initiated into the "Ancient Order of Mud Hens."

During the week, Starke commuted to Brooklyn, and his weekends were devoted to his family and sailing. He also encouraged the Bellport Bay Yacht Club to build Blue Jays, creating a racing class for youngsters. His son Bob, a financial consultant, said, "He knew the bay like the back of his hand. He loved Brookhaven, the salt marshes, the bay, the change of seasons."

Retiring from the plastics business at age 70, Bob continued working as a salesman until he turned 75. He continued a life of involvement in the community, serving as president of the Brookhaven Village Association, a Brookhaven Library Trustee, and longtime member of the Bellport Bay Yacht Club.

A constant theme in Bob's family is that he would do anything for his children. His son John said, "He didn't like hunting, but would take us because we were interested." His son Bill, who works for U.S. Fish and Wildlife, remembers a tree house built in the back yard, "just for us." In addition to his five offspring, Bob is remembered fondly by 11 grandchildren.

His daughter Jane, a nurse, came up with a fond memory. She said, "I will always remember the first beach day of the season. We would sail to Old Inlet in the

Elvira. Dad would wait for me while I changed in the women's court. Then he would take my hand while he boys ran ahead up the boardwalk to the beach."

A community ceremony of remembrance took place on July 22 in a field of flowers behind the Starke home. The old sailor would probably be pleased to hear a reading from Tennyson's "Crossing the Bar:"

"Twilight and evening bell,
And after that the dark,
And may there be no sadness of farewell,
When I embark..."

Dudley Norton: An Abundant Life

"I'm not prepared for this," said Tim Norton as he added his sometimes humorous, ineffably loving testimonial to the voices of other speakers at the memorial service held for Dudley W. Norton of Brookhaven hamlet on Sunday, a service so well attended that it was in itself a testament to the man and his life.

Wearing his father's Cornell University tie, Norton referred to the ubiquitous food stains and memorable lunches with his father, saying, "He always had a way of making us laugh, so have a laugh for Dad, and when you think of him, be happy."

Sharon Norton Remmer had begun the litany of praise for her father: "Dad always said, 'self-praise stinks,' a saying he got from his father. So often we heard from someone else about a kindness he had bestowed. My father was a philanthropist; he didn't contribute money, but countless hours of time, energy, and expertise to friends, family, and the community. We will always remember his enjoyment of the water, sailing, hiking, frozen Milky Ways, Hagen-Daaz ice cream, how much he enjoyed going to the Memorial Day Parade, and his eleven plus years of recovery. He told me recently, 'I consider myself a rich man.'"

Dudley Norton, quintessential family man, engineer, and hospital trustee died suddenly on February 20 at the age of 63, less than a week after his birthday and a few weeks after the death of his close friend, Louis Pfeiffle.

Longtime residents of Bayport, Norton's father and uncle founded Norton Brothers, Consulting Engineers and Land Surveyors in 1926, with offices in Sayville and Patchogue. Dudley Norton attended the Bayport Schools, and upon graduation, went to Cornell University, where he was awarded an engineering degree in 1957. Following his graduation, Norton was commissioned in the Civil Engineer Corps of the U.S. Naval Reserve, and served a two-year tour of duty as Assistant Public Works Officer at the U.S. Naval Air Station at Subic Bay in the Philippines. Upon leaving the service, he joined the family firm, and became its sole proprietor in 1972.

Norton was also on the Board of Directors of the former Union Savings Bank and former chairman of the Board of Directors of Brookhaven Memorial Hospital Medical Center. In addition, he was, at various times, a library trustee, a member of the New York State Board for Engineering and Land Surveying, a member of the Nassau-Suffolk Civil Engineers, and a member of the New York State Association of Professional Land Surveyors, serving as director for three terms.

In spite of his extensive involvement with the community, "He always had time for the family," said his daughter Leane Roach. Speaking in the family living room a few hours before the service that took place in the church across the street, his wife Sylvia Norton and her children spoke of the man they knew and loved. They recalled how he built a geodesic dome in the back yard, taught them how to splice lines for their boats, and dressed up as the Easter Bunny for what was to become an annual tradition. There were memories of their father riding his bike to Montauk, then calling for their mother to come out and get him, family outings to the beach, sitting with his beloved dog Okie in front of the fireplace.

Peter Paige, a friend and fellow hospital trustee for many years, said, "I remember the summer evenings our families spent together at the beach. I think he was happiest then, sitting on his boat, watching a sunset."

For his service to the hospital, Dudley Norton was presented with the coveted Teddy Roosevelt Award by the medical center and the Nassau-Suffolk Hospital Council.

Dudley Norton is survived by his wife Sylvia; his children, Sharon Remmer, Nathaniel, Leane Roach, Alisa Sinkoff, Elinor Link, Dudley W. Jr., and Timothy; his mother Helen K. Norton; his sisters, Elinor Norton, Nathalie Lewis, and Kay Hart; and nine grandchildren. The family requested that contributions in Dudley Norton's memory be made to the Brookhaven Memorial Hospital.

In the memorial service, Elinor Link read the day's Meditation from the book "One Day at a Time:"

"Love the busy life, it is a joy-filled life. I pray that I may live an abundant life." Considering the life and times of Dudley Norton, and viewing the hundreds of people who turned out on Sunday to wish him and his family clear sailing, it would appear that he lived a very abundant life indeed.

Agnes Macey

Concerning matters of grammar, she was never wrong.

Staff members, readers, and friends were saddened last week to learn of the passing of Agnes Macey, former proofreader at the Long Island Advance.

"Ms. Macey," as she liked to be called, worked as a proofreader in the Patchogue office of the Advance from 1972 until 1994. Former editor Don Moog said, "Agnes was a joy to work with. She was a professional, painstaking about her work, a stickler about split infinitives."

Moog said that he viewed Agnes not only as a co-worker, but as a friend. He added, "She was hardly ever absent and worked long hours, reading copy and the legal advertisements. We could always depend on her."

Advance publisher John T. Tuthill III said, "Agnes has been sorely missed since she had to leave us due to ill health. Her dry wit, intelligence, and meticulous proofreading set a standard in this office that was a hard act to follow."

Another friend and sometime employer, Mark Barton of Bellport, said, "We met Agnes when one of our children went to a nursery school in Patchogue, where she worked as a teacher's assistant. My wife Lois encouraged her to use her talents more fully, and she applied for a job as a proofreader. On many occasions she continued to help us out as a babysitter, pet companion, house sitter. We were good friends for 40 years."

Lois Barton said, "Agnes was a family friend. She always had a wry sense of humor, and was a gold mine of information regarding Patchogue. She was extremely generous, especially for a person of modest means. She made regular contributions to UNICEF, American Indian organizations, the NAACP, the Cancer Fund."

Agnes's son Arthur said, "My mother truly enjoyed going to Syracuse basketball and football games, she was a real fan. The last time we were together was when we saw Syracuse play Seton Hall."

Agnes's sister, Ruth Rawley of Baldwin, said, "Agnes and I loved to roam around Long Island, especially to places like Sag Harbor. Up until a couple of years ago, we took an annual trip to Vermont to visit a favorite aunt, who died at 102 last year. Agnes loved visiting historic homes and eating at the Skyline Diner near Marlboro."

Rawley noted that her sister was extremely well-educated, and was always very proud of the academic achievements of her son, a graduate of Syracuse University. Macey attended Wellsley College, graduated with a degree in psychology from Goucher College, and spent three years sin a graduate program at Johns Hopkins University, studying political science.

Agnes Macey was born in 1919 in Holtsville, and grew up on the grounds of the Suffolk Sanitarium in Selden (currently the main campus of Suffolk County Community College), where her father, Dr. Edwin Kolb, was the medical superintendent. After college, Agnes married Philip Macey, an

RAF navigator who became the chief engineering officer for the North Atlantic Division of what is now British Airways. The couple resided in Bristol, England. Philip Macey died in 1950, and his wife and small child took up residence with her family in Patchogue. Shortly thereafter, Agnes Macey started working as a teacher's assistant at the nursery school at the foot of South Ocean Avenue.

Agnes Macey is survived by her son Arthur of Patchogue, a sister, Ruth Rawley of Baldwin; grandchildren Kimberly Anne and Gregg, a nephew, James Rawley, a diplomat with the UN in Burma, and nieces Dr. Ann Rawley and Ruth Cudney of California.

Consistent with her love of learning, Agnes Macey had instructed that upon her death her remains be donated to the University of New York at Stony Brook for medical education.

Until that time, friends, relatives, and co-workers may find comfort in the thought that Agnes died shortly after attending a Syracuse basketball game with her son on January 29, 1997, a game that Syracuse won, 93-90.

Memories of Cindy Sims

"She ran with her heart," said Cindy's high school track coach Tony Toro, reflecting on the shining season that was Cindy's last year in high school.

The girl who was to become a mother of two and art teacher at a nearby high school, ran with teammates who had started a track career with her in the sixth grade, culminating in three winning seasons as the same team compiled a 6-0 record in cross country in the fall, were league champions in winter track with a record of 7-0, and placed second in the league in the spring with a 6-1 record. Cindy was named to the All-League Cross Country Team.

Toro said, "She was a hard worker, a very conscientious person. We've lost a member of our family."

In truth, most of Toro's runners have made up a kind of extended family, and many of the team members from that glorious season have kept in touch with each other, as well as the other track coaches who worked with them.

Chris Podosek, who was a junior at the time, said, "We were brothers and sisters who ran together since the sixth grade." Matt French, another junior at the time, said, "We all ran together all the time. Cindy had a truly sweet personality whose smile lit up a room. Coach Toro took us on a camping trip to Maine before Cindy's last season, and we have a movie of everybody running up there."

Another runner, Royal Hawkins, took Cindy to the senior prom at Felice's in Patchogue. "We had a great time, and after the prom, a bunch of us went down to Great Adventure the day after."

Gary Liguori, a long distance star who dated Cindy until they broke up in the middle of her senior year, said, "We were pretty close throughout high school. We had stopped dating around Christmas, but were good friends. I had no problem with her going to the prom with Royal. We were all friends. When we were going together, Cindy and I would ride bikes either to the ocean or the sound. We would go there, just sit on her Dad's boat and watch the water."

Liguori, a professor in the Exercise Science Department at the University of Wyoming, had a recollection of another good time. "My older brother Dave and Tom Hamilton took us all to the Hamptons one summer to watch the "Rocky Horror Picture Show." Cindy really got a kick out of that. Then, a year later, Coach Toro took us all to the show again. This time, Cindy got all dressed up in an outrageous costume, and really got into the spirit of things. She enjoyed life."

One of Cindy's best friends in high school was Kristin Niebuhr Schulman, who said,"We knew each other since the second grade, but became good friends when we got to high school. Cindy and I would always load up on food, then go out to the beach at Smith Point and run it off. We called her 'Bubbles,' because of her high voice and constant giggles. She was a good friend, she would do anything for anyone. She was one of the first in our crowd to drive. She had an old, black,

Chevy pickup truck she got before her senior year, and she drove us all over the place."

Schulman, who works on Wall Street, added, "I remember her loopy penmanship, with big capitals and flowing letters. It was very artistic, as she was."

A look at the1983 high school yearbook says something about Cindy and her class. The class slogan, "In touch," reflects the closeness of the class, and former teachers have commented on the unity of that particular group. The ends sheets show a pair of baby shoes, a teddy bear, and a box of M&M's, symbols of the innocence of those years. On the cross country page, there is a shot of Cindy, leading the pack in a race, and another of her standing with the team, gold medals draped around their necks. On the winter track page, there is a picture of Cindy with Gary, both smiling at the camera. On the Student Council page, Cindy, the secretary of that organization, is sitting on a bench with her friend Kristin.

It was the year of "E.T," "Cats," "Sophie's Choice," and "Fast Times at Ridgemont High." It was also the year that Cindy exhibited her work in the spring art festival and performed with the concert band, playing the French horn as she had for the past four years.

We suppose that everyone's senior year in high school is special in some way, and Cindy's year was probably not that much different than many others, yet there was a spirit of optimism during that time, The smiling faces in the yearbook look to the future with hope and anticipation, as the graduates are about to enter a rite of passage, never to return to the innocence of that last year in high school, that shining season in the sun.

There is nothing quite so tragic as a young life cut short. One morning before she was about to set off for work as an art teacher, Cindy left her children and husband and went off for a morning run along a favorite trail through the woods near her house, a trail where she was found later, murdered.

We like to think that Cindy may still be running somewhere, maybe in the Elysian fields, listening to the cheers of a celestial crowd.

Claire Shellabarger

"Claire Shellabarger was the most thoughtful, kindest man I knew," said the Right Reverend Herbert Thompson, Bishop of the Diocese of Southern Ohio and former pastor of Christ Episcopal Church in Bellport.

Rev. John Coakley, who succeeded Thompson and has since retired, said, "Claire enjoyed people a great deal. At one time or another, he was the church treasurer, vestryman, perennial ticket taker at our annual lobster dinners, and a lay reader for many years."

Jean Coakley added, "As a lay reader, he traveled regularly to the Yaphank infirmary to conduct the morning prayer sessions. He had a wonderful, quiet sense of humor once you got to know him."

The retired senior scientist from Brookhaven National Laboratory also enjoyed delivering Meals on Wheels, and was disappointed when the later stages of Alzheimer's disease prevented him from participating in that activity.

After his retirement from Brookhaven National Laboratory in 1989, Claire and his wife Marilyn traveled extensively, visiting such locales as Hawaii, China, New Zealand, Burma, Australia, Europe, Africa, Israel, Jordan, and the Artic circle.

Clair J. Shellabarger, Ph.D., senior scientist, father, husband, lay reader, world traveler, and humanitarian, died on March 12 in Rockville, Maryland. He was 73.

Not only was the life of Clair Shellabarger marked by good deeds; he was also a distinguished scientist, researcher, and teacher.

After graduating with a BA degree in zoology from Miami University in Oxford, Ohio, Claire Shellabarger, entered the U. S. Army and became a pilot, serving with the U.S. Army Air Force in Europe during World War II.

After the war, he returned to the academic life, and earned a master's degree in zoology and a Ph.D. in endocrinology from Indiana University.

He lectured and served on the staff of a number of colleges and universities, including Adelphi, Indiana, Michigan, and the state University of New York at Stony Brook.

Clair Shellabarger first worked at BNL in 1952, joining the staff of the medical department. He left in 1960 for the University of Michigan, where he was a professor of zoology. He returned to the BNL medical department in 1968, taking the post of senior scientist. During his time at the lab, he served as assistant chairman, head of the Radiobiology Division, and coordinator of the Genetics and Biochemical Sciences Program. In his final years, he headed up the Medical Department.

During his career, Shellabarger served on a number of significant committees, including the review committee of the American Cancer Society, the Life Sciences Study Team for Assessmentin Ecological Impacts of the Space Shuttle, the National Cancer Institute ad hoc Working Group on the Risks Associated with Mammography in Mass Screening for the detection of Breast Cancer, and the National Council on Radiation Protection and Measurements.

He was a member of the Radiation Research Society, the Endocrine Society, Sigma Xi, and the American Physiological Society.

Claire is survived by his wife Marilyn, three children: Charles, Nancy, and Mary; and two grandchildren. A memorial service was held at Christ Episcopal Church in Bellport.

The Reverend John Coakley

John Coakley was a man of many parts: an art student who became a demolitions expert, a husband who became a father, an art teacher who became a priest.

He is remembered by his daughter Ellen as the man who taught her how to skate on the frozen canals of Squassux Landing, the man who watched the Westminster Dog Show with her as they made crab puffs for the church social, the man who did not embarrass her when he said the benediction at her high school graduation, the man who told her not to cry as he performed her marriage ceremony.

He is remembered by a wife who saw him through a mid-life career change, who helped him through Greek, Latin, and Hebrew, and took pride in his success with theological history, an ability which was to figure prominently in his sermons. Jean Coakley said, "The most important thing in his life was to become a priest."

He is remembered by his legion of acolytes, drafted from Sunday School, to whom he introduced the mysteries of church ritual.

He is remembered by his students and fellow teachers at the Frank P. Long Elementary School. His wife said, "Those who knew him in the context of the faculty room or as part of the church family knew that his quick, dry wit and fine sense of humor were an integral part of his personality."

Marilyn Shellabarger, a former vestry member and close personal friend of the family, said, "John was extraordinarily faithful about visiting housebound parishioners and hospital patients." Another vestry member and friend, Alonso Rand, said, "It always impressed me that he was able to make everyone feel a part of the church family, and make each family feel as if he were a member of their family. He was very encouraging about participation in the church, and increased the number of lay readers significantly."

Another friend said, "When it came to old movie stars, European royalty, and history, he was never wrong." John Coakley's encyclopedic knowledge of history and sense of humor often found their way into his art, much of which adorns the walls of many houses from Bellport to East Hampton.

The Reverend John G. Coakley, 68, retired Episcopal priest, died of cancer at home in East Hampton on Sunday, August 17. Before retirement, he served as rector of Christ Church in Bellport from 1979 until 1993. He is survived by his wife Jean, a daughter, Ellen Russell of Bellport, and a brother, William D. Coakley of Westford, Massachusetts.

At the encouragement of the former rector of Christ Church, the Right Reverend Herbert Thompson, John Coakley attended Virginia Theological Seminary, where he received an MA in Divinity in 1977. After graduation, he served as chaplain at St. Mary's and as deacon at the Cathedral in Garden City. In addition, he taught at the Cathedral School.

In turn, Father Coakley continued the thread of inspiration, encouraging the vocation of his friend Keith McKenna, a deacon who served on the staff of Suffragen Bishop Catherine Roskam.

After earning his BA from the Massachusetts College of Art, Fr. Coakley received a master's degree from Harvard. He served in the U.S. Army as a demolitions expert in 1950-52 at the Aberdeen Proving Grounds in Maryland and overseas in Germany.

The family requested that in lieu of flowers, donations be made to either the scholarship fund of an Episcopal seminary or the John Coakley Memorial Fund at Christ Episcopal Church.

A Veteran's Day Story

When Richard Kaler was growing up in Patchogue, going from his mother's boarding house on South Ocean Avenue to play air rifle war in the woodsy swamp near Rider Avenue with his friend Ed Brown, he probably had no idea that the game would become a reality in the jungles of far-off South Vietnam.

Born in 1943, Kaler was a very popular member of the Patchogue-Medford High School Class of 1962, wearing his signature jacket emblazoned with the word "King," playing tackle on the football team for four years, and starring as a member of the track team for three years. He also participated in the Varsity Club, the Industrial Arts Club, and the Science Club. Under his picture in the yearbook, there is the legend: "I am as strong as a bull moose."

That strength would serve him well when he ran every day to lose weight and get in shape for the U.S. Marine Corps. Kaler's nephew, Robert Kaler of Bayport, showed a video of his uncle in Vietnam, cavorting with his buddies during an interval between battles. Kaler is holding a fellow Marine, who is standing on his shoulders. Tom Murphy, who knew Kaler as a boy, said, "He was a quiet, gentle giant."

Kaler would go on to distinguish himself in Operation Hastings, a qualified success in that it pushed the North Vietnamese Army forces back across the Demilitarized Zone. Kaler would be involved in twelve major operations within a twelve-month period, the final occurring in an area called "Helicopter Valley" in July, 1966, forty-one days before Kaler was scheduled to return home.

The following description is from the report of Operation Hastings, mentioned in the film Full Metal Jacket: "During the operation, which included search and destroy missions, members of one platoon of Company H were fired upon, and the point man was hit and killed by machine gun fire. Lance Corporal Richard Kaler immediately moved forward through he heavy fire and carried the fallen Marine back. The next day, Kaler's platoon re-engaged the machine gun position and took heavy casualties. Several Marines were pinned down by machine gun fire. Kaler then advanced and exposed himself to intense fire as he charged the enemy position. Wounded in the thigh, he silenced one enemy position before being mortally wounded. He was credited by his actions with saving many of his fellow Marines and was awarded the Navy Cross."

Unfortunately, that Navy Cross, the Marine equivalent of the Medal of Honor and the highest decoration bestowed by the Navy, never made it back to Patchogue. Forty-five years after Kaler was killed, Tony Schiozzi, a Vietnam Army veteran was researching awards and citations given to local veterans, and found that Kaler's headstone in Cedar Grove Cemetery showed that he had received the Purple Heart, but not the Navy Cross. Working with Staff Sgt. John Gallagher, a Marine recruiter stationed in Patchogue at the time, Schiozzi, along with state Senator Lee Zeldin (R-Shirley), Assemblyman Dean Murray (R-East Patchogue), and Senator Kirsten Gillibrand (D-N.Y.), pushed for a new headstone from the federal Department of Veterans Affairs.

The state Division of Military and Naval Affairs awarded Kaler with two medals: the Conspicuous Service Cross and the Conspicuous Service Star in July, 2011.

Arrangements were made to present Kaler's family with his Navy Cross posthumously on Friday, Nov. 11, at 1:30 at the North Shore University Hospital Rosen Family Wellness Center in Manhasset. This ceremony was followed by the placement of a new headstone in Cedar Grove Cemetery in Patchogue on November 19, at 12:00 p.m.

Louis A. Pfeiffle

There are certain members of the community who so distinguish themselves by their good works and leadership that the world is somehow diminished by their passing. Such a man was Louis A. Pfeiffle.

The retired president of Rollic, Inc., a family business established by his father Alexander Pfeiffle in the early 1930's with plants in Patchogue, North Carolina, and Virginia, Louis Pfeiffle was the epitome of the community activist. He was a volunteer firefighter and life member of the North Patchogue Fire Department, past president of the Patchogue Chamber of Commerce, former chairman of the Board of Directors of Brookhaven Memorial Hospital, past director of the Brookhaven Town YMCA, former president of the Patchogue Rotary Club, former president of the Nassau-Suffolk Hospital Association, former chairman of the Suffolk Community College Foundation, past member of the Industrial Development Agency for the Town of Brookhaven, chairman and director of the Union Savings Bank, and former Brookhaven Town Councilman.

In 1970, Louis Pfeiffle received the rarely-given Teddy Roosevelt Award for distinguished volunteer service to

Brookhaven Memorial Hospital, where he was a director for 16 years, serving as president for four years, and in 1981, given the Long Island Distinguished Leadership Award.

The man who touched so many lives and contributed his time to so many causes died on February 3 at his home in Blue Point after a long bout with cancer. He was 62.

Beyond the awards and official recognition, Lou Pfeiffle will be remembered by his associates and friends as a devoted family man who lived a full and joyous life, a man who enjoyed fishing, boating, and golfing at the Bellport Country Club and the Boca Raton Golf and Tennis Club, playing in the "low 80's," according to a family member.

His daughter Karen Macielak said, "He loved to spend time with his grandsons, and built a playground in the backyard called 'Alex's Park' for his first grandson. Last Christmas, he had a custom set of golf clubs made for Alex, age 7."

Pfeiffle's son Jeffrey said, "My father represented a unique balance: he was very worldly, traveling on business, but also a small-town guy. He loved marching, and played the saxaphone with the fire department band."

Dr. George Becker. a lifelong friend who went to Dartmouth with Pfeiffle, said, "Lou and I have known each other for 45 years, as classmates, roommates, fellow baseball team members, where Lou played right field and batted .300, and as fraternity brothers. We were in each other's wedding party. He was the kind of man whose friendship was always with you, when things were darkest, and when it was time to rejoice in triumph."

Hedy Felice, relative and neighbor, said, "When we had the fire (at Mickey Felice's by the bay), Louis was the first person to step forward with offers of help." She added, "In

1980, when the Patchogue Ambulance Company had a fatal accident, Louis quietly formed a committee with other local businessmen to raise funds for a new ambulance."

Louis Pfeiffle is survived by his wife of 40 years, the former Joanna Felice, whom he met in the eighth grade in the Patchogue school system. His son said, "She was playing the cello in the school orchestra, and it was love at first sight." Pfeiffle is also survived by his son Jeffrey, a daughter Kimberly, daughter Karen Macielak and her husband Paul, two grandsons Alexander and Maxwell, brothers Richard and Kenneth, a sister, Jane Hastings, and his mother, Carrie Pfeiffle.

According to the family, one of Pfeiffle's favorite hymns, "The Battle Hymn of the Republic," a song the family learned on many auto rides around the island, will be played at the funeral recessional. Interment followed in the family plot in Holy Sepulchre Cemetery in Coram. The family has requested that contributions in memory of Louis Pfeiffle be made to Brookhaven Memorial Hospital.

Thus Louis Pfeiffle died as he lived, surrounded by a loving and devoted family, listening to a favorite marching song, and urging contributions to his local hospital.

Betty Puleston

When Betty Puleston met her husband Dennis at a sailing race near Rye, New York, she was in the water, having fallen overboard. Dennis, ever the gentleman, jumped from the officials' boat to save her. He said, "How are you?" She replied, "How are you?"

Betty was impressed with the dashing naval architect and yachtsman who was to sail the South Seas, dine with cannibals, and dally with Samoan maidens, as revealed in his book Blue Water Vagabond. When they married in 1939, she thought she might be going on similar jaunts around the world with her husband.

However, that dream was to be put on hold for awhile. There was a war going on, and her husband was developing an amphibious landing craft that would be used in Okinawa and the Normandy Landing.

Betty and her husband, who had taken a job with Brookhaven Laboratory after the war, moved to a compound in the Hamlet of Brookhaven and proceeded to raise a family of four children, born three years apart: Dennis Edward, Jennifer, Pete, and Sally.

While her husband was establishing himself as a naturalist, author, artist, and founding chairman of the Environmental Defense Fund, Betty pursued her own interests. She and Helen Stark started a play school for local children. When some local youngsters were breaking windows in the Brookhaven railroad station, Betty founded the Junior Village Association. Soon she and the youngsters were replacing the broken windows, and went on to plant trees at Squassux Landing. Offering pony rides and puppetry, the Cub Scout leader began to attract youth from the surrounding area.

The Puleston compound became a hub of creative energy, intellectual activity, and social interaction. Betty would take a group of youngsters from the country and introduce them to the city, going to museums and Central Park. Then she would take a group of inner city children and bring them out to the country for pony rides and puppet shows. Betty and Bob Starke held several horse shows, complete with an announcer from Madison Square Garden. During the International Year of the Child, Betty provided space and facilities for the birth of Common Thread, a banner-making project inspired by artist Michael Ince that would spread around the world and end with a presentation at the United Nations. In later years, refugees from Sierra Leone, Croatia, and other countries would be invited to spend time at the Puleston compound.

Along with the refugees from other countries and children from North Bellport and Harlem, another group found their way to Betty's home. Led by George Stoney, whom Betty had met many years before at the Henry Street Settlement House in New York City, there were Milos Forman and Ivan Passer from Czechoslovakia; Colin Lowe, Dalton Muir, and many others from the National Film Board of Canada.

After her children had grown, Betty finally got to travel the world with family friend and documentary filmmaker George Stoney, working on various projects that more often than not had a social context: planned parenthood in India and China, educational reform in Brazil, representing the USIA in Nigeria, Turkey, and Mexico, helping people with special needs in Appalachia.

Betty and Lynne Jackson produced a film called "Race or Reason: The Bellport Dilemma," which was screened at the Museum of Modern Art in New York, and was shown locally at the Old South Haven Presbyterian Church on June 8.

In 1970, there was an outbreak of hostilities between African-American and white students at Bellport High School that forced school officials to call in the police and close school for over a week. Betty opened her home to students and their parents, giving them a place to air their grievances. Video cameras were used to facilitate dialogue. At the time, Betty described the use of video as "a way for people to get to know each other better." In the following weeks, teams of youths interviewed neighbors from the community, which would be played back to residents to other parts of town. Thus a dialogue was established. A meeting was held at a local church, sponsored by the Better Relations Committee for Constructive Action, a group of about thirty high schools students that had grown out of the meetings held at Betty's house.

In 1996, Betty donated the use of land and equipment to the Hamlet Organic Garden, a cooperative farm that has enriched the lives of many local families. She also served as a Chairperson for her alma mater, The City and Country School in New York.

On Tuesday morning, April 28, this generous woman with a great laugh and an amazing hug, this woman who liked to talk to strangers, this woman who opened her home and her heart to the world, took her final trip at the age of 91. At her side were her family, and her life-long friend George, who had taken the last train out of New York that night to be with her at the end.

Betty is predeceased by her husband Dennis, who died in 2001 at the age of 95, and their first-born, archaeologist Dennis Edward, who died when he was struck by lightning on top of El Castillo pyramid at Chichen Itza, Yucatan in 1978. She is survived by two daughters, Jennifer Clement of Brookhaven, and Sally McIntosh, of New Brunswick, Canada, and a son, Pete, also of New Brunswick, seven gifted and talented grandchildren, and seven great grandchildren, who will no doubt make their mark on the world. She is also survived by two sisters, Nancy Lee of Bellport, and Patricia Barron, of S. Dartmouth, Massachusetts.

One of Betty's favorite stories was the Grimm Brothers' tale of the stone soup. In the story, some travelers come to a village during a famine, carrying an empty pot. The villagers are unwilling to share any of their food. The travelers fill the pot with water, and drop a large stone into it and place it over a fire in the village square. One of the villagers asks the travelers what they are doing, and are told they are making stone soup, which would taste better if it had a little garnish and spices. The villagers begin to come forward with ingredients for the soup, and finally a delicious meal is enjoyed by all. The moral: By working together, with everyone contributing what they can, a greater good is achieved. Betty lived by this principle.

A "stone soup" celebration of Betty's life was planned for May 23 at the Puleston compound. Perhaps her life and times may be summed up by the words of a poet, who said, "Let me live in a house by the side of the road and be a friend to man."

Remembering George Stoney

The obituary in the New York Times was all about the professional accomplishments of George Stoney, who died recently at the age of 96. He was lauded as a documentary filmmaker, public access TV visionary, and teacher of filmmaking at NYU from 1971 until 2010.

About public access cablevision, he said, "We look on cable as a way of encouraging public action, not just access. It's how people can get information to their neighbors and celebrate the ordinary things people do to help one another."

Many people in the area remember a different George Stoney, a kind, generous, friend who contributed to the community in many ways, mostly through his enduring friendship with the Puleston family of Brookhaven.

According to Jennifer Puleston Clement, George Stoney met Betty Puleston at the Henry Street Settlement House in the early 30's, working with underprivileged children. The friendship grew, and George, who had three young children of his own in the early 60's, brought them out to the Puleston compound in Brookhaven for the summers. George would take his children and others from the neighborhood to Smith Point to go swimming, and in the evenings he would help

Betty to write grant proposals for the Meadow Lane Players, a local community theater for children featuring dance, music, and puppetry. The Meadow Lane Players evolved into the Pumpkin Patch Players, another program for children in the area, directed by neighbor Debbie Mayo.

Jennifer Clement said, "George was a great networker. He would bring many talented people out from the city to work with the kids."

In 1970 fights between black and white students at Bellport High School forced school officials to call in the police to restore order and close down the school for the rest of the day. There were other heated confrontations in the community. Several weeks after the January outbreak of hostilities, about ten high school students and twenty adults from the community met at the home of Betty Puleston. During their talks, a video tape recorder supplied by George Stoney hummed quietly in the corner. A camera was passed from one participant to another, as everyone, black or white, got a chance to express their feelings.

This initial effort led to further gatherings among other students and adults. Their efforts culminated in a film by Betty Puleston and Lynn Jackson, "Race or Reason: the Bellport Dilemma," which was shown at a tribute to George at the Museum of Modern Art recently.

The film is available at the Brookhaven Free Library, along with two other works by George about the artistry of his friend Dennis Puleston called "Autumn Flight" and "Painting from Nature."

Recently, the Plaza Cinema Arts Theater in Patchogue was named after George.

The son of a minister, George said, "I was raised to read the Bible in the morning and Shakespeare at night." George's mother died when he was six, and although he was not active in the church, he was influenced by the ethical values of the local Moravian community. After selling magazines as a boy, he took his savings of $47 and enrolled at the University of North Caroline at Chapel Hill, where he majored in English and history. After college, he became a journalist, and worked for a newspaper in Raleigh. Far away places beckoned, and he joined the merchant marines, sailed to Rio, and finally landed in New York, where he freelanced for the New York Times.

Drafted at the beginning of WWII, George went to England as part of an Air Force photo reconnaissance unit. While in England, he met his wife. After the war, he spent some time with the National Film Board of Canada, then returned to England, where he began his teaching career at Oxford. Returning to the states, he made the film All My Babies, notable for his sensitivity about such issues as race, class, and gender. In 2002 the film was added to the National Film Registry of the Library of Congress, a list that essentially defines the American film canon.

In the last 60 years, the peripatetic George Stoney could be found anywhere in the world, often accompanied by his friend Betty Puleston, devoting their efforts towards planned parenthood in India and China, educational reform in Brazil, living conditions in Appalachia, often promoting public access television and exploring other social issues. However, he would always return to Brookhaven, walking to the local delicatessen to pick up the Sunday Times, attending the Christmas services at the Old Southaven Presbyterian Church, which he formally joined two years ago, driving with Betty in a golf cart to see the spring garden of the Sack-Loves. Debbie Sack-Love said, "Every Christmas they would send us an amarylis plant in appreciation."

Also at Christmas, George and the Pulestons would sponsor an annual sing along for the neighborhood, featuring cider and cookies. A few months later, there would be the annual George and Betty Birthday party, open to the community. Betty's birthday was June 11, and George's was July 1. Debbie Mayo, who directed the Pumpkin Patch Players, said that her group would perform at the birthdays much to George's delight.

According to Jennifer Clement, "we always celebrated their joint birthday the last Saturday in June." At this year's party, Betty, of course, was not present, as she had died in 2009. Speaking to the friends and family who attended last month, George said, "I hope you all can be here next year." On that day, many of us will be there in spirit, thinking of the extraordinary life of George Stoney and his friends in Brookhaven.

George is survived by a son, James; a daughter, Louise; a sister, Elizabeth Segal; and predeceased by a daughter, Cashel (Katie). A memorial service is planned to take place in New York City on August 6.

Thelma Vaz

While many people her age would rather sit back and watch television, Thelma Vaz of Brookhaven Hamlet chose to lead a life marked by service to others. When she was named as the Long Island Advance Woman of the Year in 2002, she said, "I can't watch TV all day. It is boring."

Thelma Vaz was a member of the St. James Episcopal Church in Brookhaven Hamlet, where she served as president of the Episcopal Church Women, a group that collects clothing and toys for families in need. She also served as the parish representative to the Family Consultation Service for the Episcopal Diocese of Long Island, and sang in the church choir.

As if that were not enough, Thelma Vaz volunteered several days a week at the Bellhaven Nursing Home and helped out at the Eastern Farm Workers organization, assisting migrant workers by providing them with food and clothing.

Born and raised on the island nation of Jamaica, Thelma was the sixth child of a family of eleven children. She became a certified teacher and accountant, and briefly served as a geriatric nurse.

She taught at the elementary school level and opened her own private school that assisted children in taking their entrance examinations to high school. She also instructed students in Pittman Shorthand.

According to her son Jim, "Grammy" was known for her delicious meals, such as Plum Pudding at Christmas and "Roly-Poly," a Jamaican pastry made with grated coconut, spices, raisins, and rolled up in a flour roll. He said, "I have recollections of our holidays in Ocho Rios, when Grandma (his father's mother) and Grammy would take us down to the bay for a quick dip and to pick up fish for breakfast."

Thelma's daughter, Marcia Goodall, said, "My mother had a deep and abiding faith, and taught us about it early. She was the ultimate teacher, following students she called her 'little babies' from the kindergarten to twelfth grade and beyond. One of her nieces became a professor at Columbia University."

Marcia Goodall added, "She had two grandchildren, and hundreds of others whom she thought of as her own."

Thelma Vaz died on March 19, 2011. She was predeceased by her husband Jim in 1994, and is survived by her son, Jim Jr., and daughter, Marcia Goodall, as well as two grandsons, Sean and Kyle, and her daughter-in-law Doreen.

A funeral service was held on March 24, 2001. The Reverend Hickman Alexandre said, "Thelma was a woman of amazing faith. Even in her illness, she displayed that faith. She was always willing to share stories of her life, and every story showed her unwavering faith in God, an example we should all look to and follow."

According to her daughter, Thelma Vaz had several favorite authors, such as Milton and Wordsworth. Perhaps the best epitaph for her life comes from Milton's "Christianity," which reads, "Servant of God, well done, well hast thou fought the better fight."

Vance Sailor

In the finite world of atoms, quarks, and neutrons, he was a giant.

Dr. Vance I. Sailor was a senior physicist at Brookhaven National Laboratory, which he joined in 1949, the year he graduated from Yale University with a Ph.D. in physics. He retired from the laboratory in 1985, after 36 years of service.

During his time at Brookhaven, Dr. Sailor was involved in research dealing with energy systems, nuclear regulation, and nuclear waste disposal. For his first assignment with the lab, he made the thermal and nuclear measurements required for starting up the Brookhaven Graphite Research Reactor in 1950. From the fifties through the seventies, he led an experimental group in neutron physics research. During the 1970s he joined the Department of Applied Science for studies related to world energy problems and energy systems. Also during this time, he served for four years as the lab's director of an international energy analysis project comprised of representatives from seventeen countries and sponsored by the International Energy Agency.

In 1981 he became the associate department chairman of the lab's Department of Nuclear Energy, overseeing low-level nuclear waste management programs and participating in risk analysis projects until his retirement. He continued to serve as a consultant to the laboratory until 1995.

Dr. Sailor was the technical advisor to the U.S. delegation to the first United Nations Conference on the Peaceful Uses of Atomic Energy, held in Geneva, Switzerland, in 1955. He served as a special BNL advisor to nuclear research centers in Turkey and Greece, and served in a simlar advisory role for other collaborative projects in Europe and Russia. He was a co-author of the report,"Cost Benefit Considerations in Regulatory Analysis," published in 1995.

Robert Bari, chairman of the Department of Advanced Technology, said, "Dr. Sailor played a major, pivotal role in the establishment and early development of our reactor safety programs in the early 1970s. The origins of our probabilistic risk assessment programs are due to his initiatives. Most especially for Vance, truth and knowledge were realities from which he never wavered."

Another associate, Herbert Kouts of Brookhaven, said, "We have gone through a number of rigorous experiences together, such as earthquakes in Istanbul, and I can certify that he was a good man in an emergency."

Dr. Sailor was born in Springfield, Missouri, and attended DePauw University in Indiana, graduating in 1943 with an A.B. in Physics. He then attended M.I.T., where he received a certificate in Meteorology in 1943. During World War II, he served as a meteorologist in the U.S. Army Air Force until1946, rising to the rank of Captain, and was stationed in Africa and the Middle East. After the war, he returned to Yale

University, where he received his master's degree and 1947 and his Ph.D. in 1949, both in physics.

Active in his community, Dr. Sailor was a founder of the Suffolk Scientists for Cleaner Power and Safer Environment, as well as the Energy Education Exponents, an organization of scientists dedicated to educating the public on energy production and consumption issues. He was also instrumental in organizing the Community Chamber Players orchestra of Bellport. He was an avid sailor.

Dr. Sailor is survived by his wife Marguerite; his daughter Nancy of Westchester; two sons, Richard and John, both of Massachusetts; a sister, Mary Lou Walbridge; and three grandchildren. Friends and professional colleagues of Dr. Sailor were received in gatherings held by the family at his home.

No doubt there is another gathering somewhere, of Isaac Newton, Alfred Einstein, Richard Feynman, and Robert Oppenheimer, waiting to welcome Dr. Vance Sailor.

Jessica Pracher

Whenever Jessica Pracher wrote to her mother, from 4-H camp or during a semester at Disney World, she would always close her letters with "You are the wind beneath my wings."

Considering the brief life of the reluctant homecoming queen and star athlete from Bellport High School, Jessica herself was the "wind beneath the wings" for many people and touched many lives during her brief stay on earth.

Voted "best looking" and "most popular" in her 1993 yearbook, Jessica was the captain and MVP of the girls' soccer team.

An aunt, Penny Scherff, said, "She was like a daughter to us, and a big sister to our children." Her husband, Larry Scherff, said,"She was an angel on earth."

To Mike Kupper of New Hampshire, Jessica represented the future: after meeting at Disney World, the two had planned to finish college together in North Carolina, where he planned to go into real estate and she would become a teacher, fulfilling the prophecy she had written in her high school yearbook, "To improve the lives of little children and become teacher of the year."

Working towards this goal, Jessica was completing a course of study at Suffolk Community College in Riverhead and working at a variety of jobs to help pay for her education. In 1995, during a world-wide talent search,she was selected by the Disney Corporation to spend a semester working and training at Disney World in Orlando, Florida.

On September 14, after a night out with her friends, Jessica Pracher died in an automobile accident.

At the wake and subsequent funeral, over 1500 friends, family, former coaches, teachers, and acquaintances from Disney as well as her various jobs came to pay their respects.

Larry Dungan, her uncle, estimates that the funeral cortege of automobiles was "two miles long."

Jessica Pracher is survived by her parents, Irene and Robert Pracher, her father by birth, Wayne Smith; a sister, Kimberly Naples; her brothers, Wayne, Joshua, and Jeremy, and her grandparents.

On the day of her funeral, for the first time in the history of Bellport High School, a minute of silence was observed by students and faculty.

The family has asked that in lieu of flowers, donations should be made to the Make-A-Wish Foundation at Disney World, so that Jessica Pracher may continue to care for the children she loved so much.

Josette Auerbach

In the 1980s and 1990s, many people in our area began traveling to different parts of the world, and in Josette Auerbach, they found a travel agent who could tell them where to go, what to see, where to stay, and where to eat. Invariably, she was right, for as the saying goes, "She had been there, and done that."

Clients and friends were saddened to hear that Josette Aurbach, inveterate traveler, owner of the Bayberry Travel Agency, and co-advisor of the Bellport-Ste. Maxime student exchange, died on Friday, November 22, after a long illness.

Born in Paris in 1936, Josette Auerbach attended school in France, and came to the United States in 1956. In 1964, she married Clemens Auerbach, a scientist at Brookhaven National Laboratories, and they have been residents of Bellport since 1965.

She started in the tourism business in 1969, working out of another travel agency, and eventuallyt opened her own business, Bayberry Travel, in 1982. She quickly established herself as a designer of interesting and innovative travel packages, and hired two associates who are still with the firm.

From 1986-96, Josette Auerbach and Barbara Weissman were co-advisors of the Bellport-Ste. Maxime sister city student exchange, and many students from both countries benefited from the experience.

Many friends have fond memories of a Bastille Day celebration held at the Auerbach residence in 1989, the bicentennial of the French Revolution.

Josette Auerbach was fond of traveling, and ventured to a number of countries and parts of the U.S. with her husband and son, Claude, who has warm memories of his last trip with his mother, a tour of the Napa Valley wineries in 1994. "She couldn't let a year go by without returning to Paris," said her husband.

Josette Auerbach is survived by her husband, Clemens; her son, Claude, and his wife Elizabeth; a sister, Colette Siegel; and her mother, Rose Henenberg.

The family has requested that in lieu of flowers, donations be sent to the American Cancer Society.

Peter Theodoropoulos

They used to call Peter's Luncheonette "the Cheers of Patchogue."

It was that kind of place, the kind of eatery where at any given lunch hour, you could bump elbows with doctors from nearby Brookhaven Hospital, local politicians, highway workers on their lunch break, retirees looking for good food at reasonable prices, with a generous portion of old world hospitality thrown in for good measure.

The plaques and trophies on the walls of the luncheonette tell a lot about the man who owned the place: on one dated 1991, "For many years of outstanding coaching and dedicated service to Youth Baseball;" also in 1991, "Sponsor Award to Youth Baseball;" there is a citation from former NY state Assemblyman William Bianchi, "for services to the community;" a proclamation from the Town of Brookhaven; another from the Patchogue Lions Club, stating "appreciation for a job well done;" and others, reading, "Brookhaven Softball Summer League Champs," "Lions Club Man of The Year, 1991-1992," and "Past President, Patchogue Lions Club, 1991-1992."

There is more to the life of Peter Theodoropoulos than pieces of wood and metal adorning the walls of the restaurant. Look for the man in the loyalty of the waitresses who worked for him so many years: Kathy, Josie, Theresa, Debbie, Anna, Beatrice, Tina. Look for the man in the comments of Nick Mokkas, former cook and new owner of the restaurant. "He was

one of the best men I ever met in my life. He helped a lot of people. He was the unofficial mayor of Patchogue. We loved him."

Peter Theodoropoulos died on Sunday, November 10, at the age of 53. He was singing songs of his homeland at the time, and that says something about the man too.

Peter Theodoropoulos was born in Greece, and came to Patchogue when he was a teenager. He worked in a variety of restaurants, the Island Grill, the Tiffany Diner, George's Restaurant, before opening his own place in 1973.

During the years that followed, the luncheonette thrived, and Theodoropoulos became notable as a real estate entrepreneur, contributing to the development of the immediate area.

He is survived by his wife Joan; two sons,Simon and Theodore; and two sisters,Tina Lee of Utah and Evthokia Papageoriou of Greece.

John Binnington, A Man of Many Parts

John Binnington, who died on August 14, was a man of many parts.

He started the Research Library at Brookhaven National Laboratories and shepherded its growth to become one of the largest scientific and technical resources on Long Island. Binnington was instrumental in establishing the Suffolk County Cooperative Library System and the Long Island Library Resource Council. In addition, he served as president of the Brookhaven Free Library Board of Trustees.

He was a founding member of the Playcrafters, an amateur theatrical troupe, and appeared in its first production, "Bell, Book, and Candle" in 1960. He appeared in a number of subsequent performances: "South Pacific," "Brigadoon," "Bus Stop," "The Little Foxes," "Sabrina Fair," and "Mr. Roberts."

The son of an Anglican priest, he was an active member of Christ Episcopal Church in Bellport, serving as choir member, vestryman, Senior Warden, and founder of the Lay Readers' Guild, an organization that still sends teams of readers to conduct services at the Yaphank Infirmary and the South Country Nursing Home. For these services to the church, he was awarded the Bishop's Cross, a rare distinction.

Born in London, England, in 1914, Binnington earned degrees from the University of the South at Sewanee, Wesleyan University, and Columbia University.He worked as a librarian at the University of Rhode Island and the U.S. Merchant Marine Academy at Kings Point before becoming an associate librarian and eventually the head of the research library at Brookhaven National Laboratory.

In 1966, Binnington was a member of a U.S. Library of Congress delegation sent to Russia to study the library system there. Afterwards, he hosted a delegation from Russia, who toured libraries in the United States.

The Binningtons were the first family to live on site at Brookhaven Laboratory, when it was established on the former grounds of Camp Upton. Binnington was active in the Employees Recreation Association, particularly in its theater group, and helped to bring world-class artists such as Pearl Bailey and Dave Brubeck to perform.

He retired from the Laboratory in 1979, to sail, to write, to travel, and to serve on various library committees.

Binnington is survived by his wife, Julia Binnington; his son, Thomas; his daughters, Bree Rice and Marjorie Braxton; his stepdaughters, Vijaya Maclean, and Loveday Kochersberger; and eleven grandchildren. He was predeceased by his first wife, Blanche, and a son, John E. Binnington.

At a service held at Christ Episcopal Church, the Right Reverend Herbert Thompson told an overflow crowd of 200 friends and family, "John gave clear instructions about this service. There will be no homily, no eulogy. We are the eulogy."

Thompson then referred to The Gospel According to St. John, reading, "There was a man sent from God, whose name was John...to bear witness of the Light, that all men through him might believe," adding, "We've come here this afternoon to say 'thank you' to God for our John."

Thompson's meditation included a poem written by John Binnington, entitled "The Leaf," which seems to sum up the many parts of the man who was a bibliophile, an actor, a father and husband, a sailor, and a man of the faith:

At last, too soon perhaps, a passing wind
Loosens my hold and down I float
To rest with others on the still green grass.
A passing poet bends, then lifts me to the sky.

There, before the sun, he sees me,
My color, my veins, my starlike shape
And knows, as my Creator knows,
That I am one small part of hope
And comfort for mankind.

Foster Hoff

The first thing you noticed about him was his height. He was about 6'4", and like many tall men, he walked with a slight stoop, but he always seemed taller than he was, larger than life. The next thing you saw were the blue eyes, with crinkles in the corners, the eyes of a man who smiled often and sincerely, the eyes of a man who cared about students and teachers alike, the eyes of a man who inspired you to do your best.

He was the first principal of Longwood High School, and there was a pioneering spirit in those early days, when one of the largest school districts on Long Island was being born. His family had a strong leadership gene: his brother was the governor of Vermont, and his son was to become a student leader at the high school.

He was the kind of principal whose door was always open, the kind of principal who spent more time out in the halls talking to students than in his office, the kind of principal who did his paperwork at home, working far into the night.

The students and faculty thought so highly of Dr. Hoff that they elected him "Principal of the Year" in a contest run by radio station WABC in New York. At that time, there were about 600 students attending Longwood, but they collected 962,000 votes on cards with Dr. Hoff's name and a signature. As the winner, Dr. Hoff received a television set and a stereo hi-fi.

Recently we were saddened to hear that Foster Hoff, a longtime resident of Patchogue, died on December 3 of complications from interstitial fibrosis at Williamsburg Community Hospital in Virginia.

Foster Hoff is survived by his wife of 51 years, Marcia Hoff; three children: David Hoff of St. Louis, Mo.; Karen R. Ott of Philadelphia; and Jeffrey H. Hoff of Charlotte, North Carolina; and six grandchildren.

Born in Turners Falls, Massachusetts, Dr. Hoff earned bachelors and masters degrees from Colgate University, and his doctorate in education from New York University. He worked in public school education from 1948 until 1988, holding positions as a math teacher in Lockport, a curriculum coordinator and vice principal at Freeport, a principal at Longwood, a superintendent at Lindenhurst, and a BOCES director of special education.

During his retirement, he pursued his passion for golf, and was a volunteer driver for the Red Cross.

As is often the case with someone who has affected us profoundly, we prefer not to think of how Foster Hoff died, but how he lived. Each June, he had a special message in the school annual for the graduating students. In 1965, he wrote: "During a lifetime, most individuals will be judged relative to their financial achievements, their professional competence, their social acumen, their marital and parental success, and ultimately, in terms of their impact upon society. Human judgment concerning life involves achievement in all areas, the talents with which the individual started, and the values employed by those rendering the judgment. Perhaps the ultimate test is the ability of each person to live effectively with himself and with other people."

It seems to me that these words are the most fitting epitaph for Foster Hoff, educator, mentor, and friend.

Audie French

When Audrey French died at the age of 82 on December 22, 1999, it shocked and saddened many people in town. She moved through life with style and grace, and somehow the village of Bellport and the larger community of Suffolk County is diminished by her passing.

Among her personal effects were the membership cards that attested to a life of activism and concern for nature and people in general: National Organization of Women, The Nature Conservancy, The Wilderness Society, Sierra Club, the Historical Society of Early American Decoration, National Trust for Historical Preservation, American Association for University Women, Bellport-Brookhaven Historical Society, League of Women Voters, Planned Parenthood, and the Museum of American Folk Art.

The list goes on and on, but perhaps the most important membership to Audie French was belonging to the National Alliance for the Mentally Ill.

Turning the mental illness of a family member into positive activism, she was president of the King's Park Chapter of NAMI for many years. After the King's Park facility closed down, she continued to conduct meetings of NAMI at Pilgrim

Psychiatric Center. In addition, she led monthly informational meetings scheduled for directors of King's Park and concerned families of the mentally ill. Ten years ago, she was one of five women who founded Park House, a community residential facility, in Smithtown. She served on the board of directors of that agency until her death.

One of her daughters, Anne Michelsen, said, "Mother had the ability to listen to people in terms of their problems. She was blind to their faults, never judgmental."

During these same years, Audrey French was instrumental in developing another site for the mentally ill, Clubhouse of Suffolk, a psychiatric rehabilitation facility patterned after Fountain House in New York City. Clubhouse recently won an award from New York State as being the "finest facility of its kind, creating a safe place for the mentally ill."

According to a family member, one of the last things Audrey French said was, "Somebody has to take over my Tuesday meeting at the Clubhouse."

In addition to testifying before county and state legislatures regarding mental health issues, Audie French was active in her community. While raising five daughters, she was instrumental in getting school crossing guards placed at the four corners in the village. With her husband, Dr. Willard French, she was a member of the local historical society, and with him, ran a number of successful antiques fairs to benefit the Brookhaven Memorial Hospital Medical Center.

A graduate of Wheaton College in 1940, Audie intended to become a teacher, but eventually wound up working for the South Country Library for 31 years, specializing in children's reading and restoring old books. She was an avid gardener and enjoyed going to the beach.

In recent years, Audie became interested in an international movement called "Creation Spirituality." According to a close friend, Catherine Kellogg, who also espoused the new cosmology that integrates scientific understanding with ancient traditions, "She believed that the most profound challenge of our time is how to maintain a livable earth, to recover the sense of the sacred in all things."

"She said that rediscovering the spirituality in creation was like coming home," Kellogg added.

Audrey French is survived by her daughter: Anne Michelsen of Brookhaven, Gail F. Enkey of Willmette, Il, Carol F. Milbury of Derry, NH, Ellen Ellsworth of Scarborough, ME, and Barbara Socha of Smithtown; eight grandchildren; and three great-grandchildren.

At her memorial service, it was noted that Audie French, who worked so hard to created a home for desperate people set loose on the streets, had, herself, come home at last. In the words of Virginia Woolf, "She found a room of her own."

Joe Adams, Photographer

Residents of Brookhaven Hamlet were saddened to hear of the passing of Joe Adams, who died at the age of 85 in his home on Friday, March 10.

Adams was the kind of photographer/journalist who devoted his life to his art. According to his son Jack, Adams once piloted a 16-foot outboard motor boat, powered by a 25-horsepower motor, from the mouth of the Carmans River on Long Island to an outdoor writers' convention in Miami, Florida. The stunt got the attention of magazine publishers, and his story, "New York to Miami in an Eggbeater," was published in Cavalier Magazine. Asked about his 2,000-mile round trip, Adams said, "I'd do it again, but not right away."

Born in Center Moriches, Adams attended high school there. Looking through a magazine in the library before graduation, he became interested in photography. After graduation in 1932, he took a correspondence course, then built a dark room in the family home on a small farm in Brookhaven.

In Brookhaven, he learned composition from a mentor, Gardner Rae, a successful cartoonist and fellow member of the Brookhaven Fire Department.

In 1940, Adams won a certificate of merit in a national newspaper snapshot contest. During the war, he worked for Pratt and Whitney in Connecticut as a paint sprayer. After the war, he had a studio in Riverhead for a time, then set up shop in his Brookhaven home.

A life member of the Brookhaven Fire Department, Adams was also at one time a photographer for the Long Island Advance and Brookhaven Memorial Hospital. Working out of his home, he became a well-known recorder of society functions. He also did campaign work for former state Assemblyman William Bianchi.

In addition, Adams was a designer and builder of light, fast boats, and on occasion sold plans and various articles about boating and fishing to such magazines as Mechanics Illustrated and Sports Afield.

Adams is survived by his son, Jack, an industrial arts teacher. He was predeceased by his wife Elizabeth and daughter, Barbara, who died four years ago. A memorial mass was celebrated at Mary Immaculate R.C. Church in Bellport, followed by Oaklawn Cemetery in Brookhaven.

Looking at the body of work compiled over the years, the weddings, celebrations, family portraits, artistic photos of Great South Bay and Carmans River, it is easy to arrive at the most appropriate epitaph for Joe Adams: he was truly a photographers' photographer.

Ruth Call

If anyone wanted to know anything about Brookhaven, our hometown, and the surrounding area, they would telephone Ruth Call, and more often than not, she would be able to tell them. She was the kind of person who lived for her family and her community.

Ruth Call, 70, died of pnuemonia on November 30, after a 26-year battle with multiple sclerosis.

Her sister, Betty Budny, said, "She took a lot of knowledge with her."

Ruth Call was a well-known authority on duck decoys, old bottles, and antiques in general. Her husband Ed, who was at her side for the long fight, said, "She dug old bottles out of everybody's back yard, from Maine to North Carolina."

Two years ago, Ruth and Ed were honored by the Long Island Decoy Collectors Association, "for starting many a new collector with a gift of a first decoy."

Ruth was known far and wide as a self-appointed mother hen. Looking at the world from her scooter, her van, and by visiting innumerable yard sales, she kept her finger on the pulse of the community, and reached out to it by way of the telephone. Often she would call the local newspaper, alerting it of a problem that needed attention.

"Anytime wanted to know something, all you had to do was call her," said her husband Ed.

Her daughter, Lynne Scheibel, said, "If you were a friend, you were a friend for life. She called people all over the country." Ed added, "Sometimes I was afraid to open the phone bill, but it that's all I had to worry about, well, it was her outlet to the world."

As with most cases of multiple sclerosis, there were good days and bad days, but Ruth spent most of them in her beloved swimming pool, heated so she could use it in any season.

Born on February 13, 1929, Ruth Call grew up on Robinson's duck farm on the Carman's River, attended a one-room schoolhouse in Southaven, and graduated from Bellport High School. She was working at Brookhaven National Laboratory when she met her husband, and eventually worked in design at the American Institute of Physics. They married in 1951, and she retired to raise a family.

Her daughter Lynne said, "We always had a houseful of kids."

"It reminded me of a fun park," her husband Ed said. "There were volleyball games on Saturday nights, cookouts on Sunday, trips to Montauk to see the sunrise, beach parties, swimming at the old mill in Southaven, and a menagerie of horses, goats, dogs, and cats to care for."

Ruth was a volunteer at Brookhaven Memorial Hospital for many years, and played volleyball in the local school gymnasium in the evenings.

When MS struck, Ruth did not withdraw from life, but she embraced it as much as she could.

Her daughter said, "She was an avid amateur photographer. As the MS progressed, she had to get a smaller, lighter camera. Then eventually, she composed the pictures in her mind, and had my father take them for her."

Ruth was also an avid bird watcher, and her husband took her down to Squassux Landing every day. "In better times," he said, "she rode down there in her motorized scooter to tell the fishermen what they were doing wrong."

Ed also spoke of the time when his wife was being treated at the University Medical Center at Stony Brook, and a specialist asked her if she would speak about MS to some young interns. "She was proud to be able to speak to them," said her husband.

Before her final illness, Ruth's last days were spent doing the things she loved best: swimming in her heated pool just before Thanksgiving; sending three prized decoys to a museum in Salisbury, Maryland; looking at the surf from the handicapped boardwalk at Smith Point; preparing for the holidays.

"She loved holidays," said her daughter Lynne. "We always got as many thoughtful gifts as we did when we were children."

In addition to her husband and her daughter Lynne, Ruth Call is survived by another daughter, Katherine Gullett of Waskom, Texas; a son, Edward Call of Warrantsville, PA; a brother, Ralph Taylor of Shirley; sister Betty Budny of Bellport; and five grandchildren.

A memorial service has been scheduled for the spring. Her daughter Lynne said, "She loved spring, when the flowers came up, it was a renewal of everything she believed in."

Ruth Call would probably want us all to remember that it's not important to note how she died, but how she lived.

Ralph Robinson

Some people are fortunate enough to live several lives during their allotted time on earth. Such a person was Ralph P. Robinson, formerly of Southaven, who died at the age of 72 in Hertford, North Carolina, on November 28, 1999.

Born on the Carmans River Duck Farm owned by his family, Robinson grew up there, swimming in the old millpond with his brother and sisters. Eventually, he and his brother worked the farm until the mid-1950s, when he had an epiphany.

According to his sister, Dorothy Redman, Robinson was disposing of some garbage late in the afternoon one day when an unopened letter fell at his feet. As the sun set over the tree tops in the west, he opened and read the letter. The fading light fell on an invitation from an East Harlem Protestant Parish, asking him if he wanted to become a lay minister and manage a camp for troubled youths in Peekskill, New York.

Leaving the farm to his brother, Robinson and his wife went upstate to work with troubled teenagers. During the years they worked up there, they adopted four children, then had two of their own, then adopted two more.

Semi-retired, Robinson and his family moved to Virginia Beach, where he worked in a paneling factory. It was there that doctors believe he was exposed to the asbestos that eventually contributed to his demise, according to the family.

While working in Virginia Beach, Robinson and his wife would take long drives in the countryside, and on one of these excursions, found Hertford, NC. According to Robinson's sister, the place was so much like Southaven that her brother fell in love with it, bought land, and built his own home.

"It was the kind of place where you had to drive 30 minutes to get to the nearest grocery store," she said.

In 1985, Robinson undertook Basic Law Enforcement training and became a Deputy and Drug Abuse Resistance Education (DARE) officer. He also worked in the Governor's One-on-One program, touching the lives of hundreds, perhaps thousands, of local youth. In August, 1998, he was appointed sheriff, then elected to that post in November of the same year.

Active in many organizations, he was a member of the Chapel on the Sound, the Hertford Rotary Club, the N.C. Sheriff's Association, and formerly served in the National Guard.

Keith Lane, Pastor of Oak Hill A.M.E. Zion Church in Hertford and one of Robinson's DARE youngsters almost ten years ago, said to the large crowd that gathered in the local high school for his memorial service, "Mr. Robinson was a brother to me. He was also like a father. We often discussed the word of God. My mother called him the smiling deputy before he became sheriff."

District Court Judgel J.C. Cole said, "Ralph Robinson faithfully carried the torch for kindness, love, and mercy, reminding us that we, too, must make it burn brightly."

It seems fitting that Ralph Robinson was eulogized in the local high school, a place where he reached out to so many troubled youngsters, offering them a smile, a handshake, and compassion. There should be more Ralph Robinsons in this world.

Frederick H. Strybing

Fredrick Strybing was a man who served his country and community well and faithfully. Dedicating his life to public service, the Patchogue High School graduate served in the U.S. Marine Corps in World War II, was a Suffolk County Police Officer for 31years, and became the Mayor of Bellport Village in 1978.

During his stint with the U.S. Marines, Fred Strybing served for 28 months in the European theater of Operations, and was a member of a light battalion sent to guard the U.S. Naval Base in Londonderry, Northern Ireland. He was honorably discharged after four years, with the rank of sergeant.

Shortly thereafter, Strybing became a patrolman for the former Brookhaven Town Police Department, and was named headquarters precinct commander after ten years. The force became part of the Suffolk County Police Department in 1960. Fred Strybing was promoted to the rank of captain, and took over the Marine Division until 1975. He retired as a Suffolk police inspector in 1977. His wife Maybelle said, "He loved his job. He felt that the police were a helping profession."

After retiring from the police force, Fred Strybing became the mayor of Bellport in 1978, but a heart ailment forced him to resign before his term was completed. After, he spent his time gardening and traveling.

At the beginning of a meeting of the Bellport village trustees, Mayor Frank Trotta eulogized Fred Strybing and dedicated the meeting to his memory. Trotta said, "We were elected as trustees when Fred became mayor. He was in office for a short time, but had a great impact on the village. He convinced us that the golf course should make money, and it has. He said the village should own its own ferryboat, and it does. This is his legacy. He treated the mayor's position as a full-time job."

Frederick Strybing, age 80, died of natural causes at home. In addition to his wife, he is survived by a son, Frederick, of California.

The man who served his country and community so well has been laid to rest in the Cedar Grove Cemetery, reminding us of a line from Robert Louis Stevenson's "Requiem:" Here he lies where he longed to be, Home is the sailor, home from the sea."

David Reay

Perhaps one measure of a man's life is the number of people who turn up at his memorial service. If the more than 200 friends and family who crowded into Christ Episcopal Church in Bellport on a Monday are any indication, David N. Reay, who died in an automobile accident at the age of 81, affected many people indeed.

As The Reverend David H. Roseberry of Plano, Texas, said in a recent interview, "David was very involved in his community. He was a loving grandparent, father,and husband. He was known for his generosity and love of life. He was devoted to his wife and children. Like many individuals described in Tom Brokaw's book, he was one of the 'great Americans' who came back from World War II to build America."

Roseberry also spoke of his father-in-law's vitality: "He once described himself as '175 pounds of beef, speed, dynamite, and destruction.' As he aged, he felt as if he was doing pretty well."

Born in Morgantown, West Virginia, in 1918, David Neville Reay grew up there, attended the University of West Virginia, and after graduation, joined the U.S. Air Force in 1939.

During World War II, he flew B-24s and B-25s, sub hunting in the Caribbean. He became a squadron commander and rose to the rank of Lieutenant Colonel.

After the war, he went to work for American Airlines as a pilot, and by the time he retired in the1960s, he had become the General Manager of Operations. He also continued to raise three children after their mother, Ruth H. Reay passed away.

In the spring of 1973, he met Mary Fox Lamson on a blind date, and they married within six months. "Foxie," as he called her, had four children by a previous marriage, so with their union, their family more than doubled.

The couple moved to Bellport in the early 1980s and opened Temperance Hall, a gallery dedicated to providing exhibition space to local artists as well as nationally known craftspeople. In addition, Reay supported his wife in her endeavors as an accomplished artist by photographing her work and providing ideas for others. The couple became active members of the Bellport Chamber of Commerce.

There followed a kind of golden semi-retirement: shows at the gallery, which had become very successful, sailing trips across the bay to Old Inlet, gardening, playing golf with one son, and going hunting with the other. Concerned about the environment, Reay showed up at almost every Carmans River protest demonstration, and worked to keep the river clean. He was on the village's Architectural Review Board, and he was elected to serve as a library trustee in 1994 and 1997. During that time, he also served on the Library Building Committee.

Pat Campbell, the library director at that time,said, "David was one of those people who seemed to always be in a state of grace. He was a very considerate, caring man, yet optimistic, down-to-earth, and fun-loving."

David Reay is survived by his wife, Mary; son, David S. Reay of Hauppauge; daughters, Margerite Rehneer of Scotia, N.Y. and Ruth V. Trachtenberg of Mountain Lakes, N.J.; stepdaughter, Frances Roseberry of Plano, Texas; stepsons Stuart Lamson of Mystic, Connecticut, Stephen Lamson of Westhampton, David Lamson of Port Jefferson, and 14 grandchildren.

The family has requested that in lieu of flowers, donations be made to the South Country Library Endowment Fund.

David Reay will be remembered for many of his accomplishments, but mainly his love for his family, his community, and his country, and as the cover of his memorial service reads, "Love endureth all things."

Frederick Irving Smith

The Reverend Frederick Irving Smith, former pastor of the United Methodist Church in Bellport, died on April 17, 1996, in Orange City, Florida.

News of his passing evoked many memories among Bellport residents: Fred Smith as firefighter with Bellport's Hook and Ladder Company, rescuing youngsters from a burning school on that fateful day in March 1963; Fred Smith broadcasting on Radio WALK, bringing comfort to shut-ins; Fred Smith as chaplain at the Brookhaven National Laboratory Hospital, easing the pain of the sick; and Fred Smith as tuba player, huffing and puffing away in the summer concerts held at the bandstand near the Bellport dock.

During his 24-year tenure at the Bellport Methodist Church, Smith served God and humanity in a variety of capacities. He did double duty as chaplain and member of the Bellport Fire Department, and was a charter member of the Bellport Ambulance Company. He was also an active member of the North Patchogue Fire Department Band.

Smith was chairman of the Suffolk County Council of Churches, and managed the scheduling of radio services held each weekday afternoon on Radio WALK. He also broadcast a program on WALK called "Religion in the News" on Sunday mornings.

Smith was instrumental in founding the Beach Ministry at Smith's Point, and later beach ministries that served cooperatively at other points on Fire Island. Another ministry he assumed was visiting and holding monthly worship services for patients at the Patchogue Nursing Home. Smith also served with the Salvation Army as welfare secretary ot the local unit for many years.

He was the chaplain for Brookhaven Memorial Hospital and the Medical Research Hospital at Brookhaven National Laboratory. In addition, Smith served as chairman of the Camp Committee for the New York Conference, was a member of the Conference Board of Education for Evangelism, and was a delegate to the World Methodist Convocation on Evangelism to Jerusalem in 1974.

The Rev. Smith was born on May 9, 1921, in Port Washington, N.Y., where he was raised. During World War II, he served in the U.S. Marine Corps for four years, with a tour of duty in the South Pacific. In 1944, he met Billy Sue Wade, a member of the Women's Reserve of the U.S. Marine Corps, at Camp Mirimar, San Diego. They were married in 1945.

After the war, Smith and his bride returned to Long Island, where he resumed his job with the Vicks Chemical Company, as well as the college education that had been interrupted by the war. Upon graduating from Hofstra University and Union Theological Seminary, Smith answered the call to ministry in 1950, and was appointed to the Bellport Methodist Church in June of that year.

After his retirement for health reasons in 1974, Smith and his wife split their time between Madison, New Hampshire, where they had a vacation cabin purchased in 1957, and their winter residence in Orange City, Florida. Since his retirement, Rev. Smith served as a minister of visitation for the Madison Baptist Church in New Hampshire, the First United Methodist Church in Deltona, Florida, and from 1982 until 1994, the Trinity United Methodist Church in Deland, Florida. He continued to play the tuba as well.

The Reverend Smith is survived by his wife Billy Sue, three children: John Smith of Bellport, The Reverend James Smith of Danville, New Hampshire, and Laurel Sue Smith of Davenport, Florida, and a brother, the Reverend Benjamin Smith of Littleton, Colorado.

Memorial services were held at the Trinity United Methodist Church in Deland, and many former Bellport residents who had retired to Florida were in attendance.

When the Reverend Frederick Smith retired in 1974, the choir composed a tribute, which read in part:

"You have been our pastor and our friend
For all these many years.
You have wedded, christened, counseled us,
Always helped to dispel our fears.
You have always answered when we called,
Always lent a helping hand
By sharing, caring, guiding us,
Or playing tuba in the band."

One may easily imagine Fred Smith playing the tuba in a celestial band somewhere.

Joe Pendergast

For many Bellporters, St. Patrick's Day just wasn't the same this year. Joe Pendergast, part leprechaun, part gadfly, and part man about town, was not there to make up a batch of Irish soda bread and marmalade, or whip up a feast of corned beef and cabbage for family and friends, as had been his custom for many years.

Joe Pendergast was proud of his Irish heritage. When he and his wife Margot went to Ireland in 1988, with one of his daughters, Kathy, and son-in-law Paul Ellis, he was the only one in the group to kiss the Blarney Stone.

Joseph Edward Pendergast died on February 23, 1998, at the age of 82. He is survived by his wife Margaret Stuart Pendergast, four children: Maryanne Pendergast of Cleveland, Kathy Pendergast Ellis, Joseph Pendergast, Jr., and Peggy Pendergast of North Shirley, and three grandchildren: Shannon, Michael, and Maeve. His family has expressed a debt of gratitude to Hospice Nurse Bill Hutton and Home Health Care Giver Susie Gambles.

Joe Pendergast was raised in Lawrence on Long Island, and as a young man during the Depression worked as a runner on the floor of the New York Stock Exchange. In 1940, he married Margaret Stuart, who was teaching in West Islip. After a stint with the U.S. Marines in World War II, Joe Pendergast moved to Brooklyn Heights, and worked as a buyer for Abraham and Strauss while attending New York University at night. In the late forties, the Pendergasts moved to Patchogue Shores, where Mrs. Pendergast's family had a summer home. Joe Pendergast began a career in advertising, working for the BBDO Agency throughout the fifties. At that time, the family moved to their home on Maple Street in Bellport. From the sixties until his retirement in the eighties, Mr. Pendergast worked as a stockbroker, principally with Janney Montgomery Scott.

Active in the community, Mr. Pendergast was the longtime treasurer of the South Bay Art Association, and will be long remembered for the parties he held after the Fourth of July Artists on the Lane show.

Pendergast was also instrumental in raising money for the construction of the community band shell in the seventies. He was a founding member of a group of retirees known as the "Baycrafters," an organization that held an ecumenical yard sale to raise money for local church food pantries. According to Larry Cummings, another member, when the group cleaned out their attics and basements, they came up with another scheme, the Brown Bag Ball, usually held in January or February. In the last nine years, the Brown Bag Ball has averaged donations of 2,000 pounds of food and about $500 a year for the local food pantries.

Interested in local politics, Pendergast gained a reputation as a "curmudgeon," said old friend Phil Munson. He attended many village board meetings, and, according to Munson, "looked out for the interests of the people, and saw himself as a member of the loyal opposition." Asked to run for mayor one year, Pendergast said, "I can do more for the people by not being mayor."

After the funeral services, there was an occasion that would have made Joe Pendergast a happy man: a gathering of friends and family at the home of Phil Munson, where everyone hoisted a glass and drank several toasts to the old Irishman.

As Joe Pendergast Jr. saluted his departed father, he quoted John Masefield's "Enslaved"

"O beautiful is love and to be free
Is beautiful, and beautiful are friends
Love, freedom, comrades, surely make amends
For all these thorns through which we walk to death.
God, let us breathe your beauty with our breath."

Thus the son marked the passage of his father, a man who lived for his family and community, a man who knew love, freedom, and comrades, a man who knew how to live life to its fullest. Such a man was Joseph Edward Pendergast.

George C. Furman

George C. Furman, patriarch of a family that had its roots in the founding of Patchogue, died on January 8 at the age of 88. On one side of the family, there were the Smiths and Conklins of early Patchogue, descended from the first fishing and farming families of Brookhaven, including the Wicks and Homans, most of whom could trace their roots back to William Brewster and the original Mayflower voyagers. Furman's father, who came from a family of fishermen out of Brooklyn, started as a clamdigger, became a school teacher, then a lawyer, and wound up as an early Suffolk County Republican leader, and ultimately a New York State Supreme Court Judge. The family grew and flourished along with the village, and eventually there was a Conklin Avenue and the Furman Building on one of the four corners at the center of Patchogue.

George Furman grew up in Patchogue, and as captain of the basketball team, he led the high school to several championships. Also in high school, he and Rupert Parks traveled to the New York State tennis championship finals in Albany. The were picked to win, according to his son, George H. Furman, but it started to rain, and Parks, who wore glasses, could not see the ball well enough to return it. Unfortunately, they lost in the finals. After graduating in 1927, Furman went on to Cornell University, where he also captained a winning basketball team. Graduating from Cornell in 1932, he went on to the Albany Law School of Union College, where he received a degree in 1934. A member of the Suffolk County Bar Association for 66 years, he served for ten years as county Assistant District Attorney, as chairman of the Brookhaven Town Ethics Board, and as a Brookhaven Town Attorney for the Assessor's Office.

Furman was the original incorporator, co-trustee with his brother Hugh S. Furman, and attorney for the Manor of St. George Museum, site of the famous Revolutionary War Battle and raid by Colonel William Tallmadge. Thanks to investments arranged by Furman, the museum is self-supporting and operates free of charge.

Until his semi-retirement, Furman was the director of the Fleet Bank of Eastern Long Island. He continued to go into his law office every day until his illness. He had been the attorney for the Banker's Trust and Company during the Depression, in charge of foreclosures, and was involved in the sale of the Bellport country club to the village.

Furman was a former president of trustees for the United Methodist Church of Patchogue. During his stewardship, he made possible the construction of the Wesley Education Wing in 1964, providing for 400 Sunday school children. In 1993, Furman was honored by the Patchogue Chamber of Commerce at their annual dinner for his ten years of service, including acting as president of that organization.

Furman is remembered by his family and friends as a fine athlete and fierce competitor. According to his son, Joel Furman, he sailed everything from a J-Class to a Narrasketuck, and he particularly enjoyed "beating the Roes." He went on to win a gold medal in the Senior Olympics, sailing a Sunfish out of Darien, Connecticut. According to his family, Furman would often go bird hunting with an old friend, Nat Norton, Sr.

In addition, he was an avid bridge player, and met weekly with the South Shore Bridge Club. Another player, John T. Tuthill, publisher of The Advance, said of Furman's game, "He was an excellent player, one of the best." According to his daughter Gail, her father played a wicked game of backgammon. "He hated to lose. If that happened, he would want to play again right away, even if it meant ending the game well after midnight." His son, George H. Furman, said, "He was well-known for bending the wickets in croquet. Besides, he was a great gambler. We enjoyed taking him to Foxwoods for his eighty-eighth birthday."

George Furman is survived by his children Joel M. Furman, Esq. of Patchogue, George Furman II of Cookeville, Tennessee, and Gail Moore of Vermont; and predeceased by his wife Marian, who died in Vermont in 1988, and his brother, Hugh S. Furman, a World War II veteran who saw action in the Normandy Invasion and the Battle of the Bulge. He is also survived by six grandchildren: George C. Furman II, Andrew W. Furman, Jacquelyn Moore, Thomas Moore, Susanne Moore, Wendy Moore; and four great-grandchildren: Zacherya Gauthier, Katie Gauthier, Allison Gauthier, Kiah-Lin Furman, and Christopher Warner.

There was a viewing at the Furman home in Bellport, and among the many pictures and mementos in the living room, there are two favorites taken in the last years: one is of George Furman in his eighties, sailing a sunfish like a teenager; the other shows Furman sitting on his lawn in September, taking great pleasure in the sight of hundreds of Optimist class sailboats as they danced across the sunlit bay during the Atlantic Coast Championships.

Mary Chavious

The ambulances moved slowly and silently through the night. They carried representatives from the Bellport, Brookhaven, and Shirley ambulance companies, and they were on their way to honor Mary Chavious, fellow ambulance volunteer, special education teacher, wife, mother, and grandmother.

At the wake, her husband Greg, ever polite and thoughtful, fought back the tears, thanked everybody for coming, and introduced their children and grandchildren to the gathering. Their marriage truly represented the diverse community in which they lived, and worked, and played.

He came from Hillborough, North Carolina, and she came from Carbondale, Pennsylvania. They met at the "40 Lanes" in Patchogue, bowling in the Bellport Teachers League. He was ebullient and outgoing, she was quiet and introspective. They were living proof that opposites attract, but what a team they made as parents, members of the ambulance company, and officers of the Teachers Association.

Her husband said, "She taught me how to deal with people who were different." He talked about how he relied on her quiet strength and non-judgmental attitude. "I would come home after a difficult ambulance meeting, and she would be my shoulder. She was a good listener."

Chavious shared a letter from a former student, Laile Fairbairn. In a letter that Mary never got to read, Laile referred to late-night debates about education and other matters, saying, "Mary was always the calm one. Every one should have a Mary Chavious in their lives."

Greg Chavious said that when his wife knew that she was too sick to continue teaching, she asked him to take her up to the Frank P. Long School one last time to speak with her students. He said, "Sitting there in her wheelchair, with her oxygen tank, she asked us to leave her alone with her students for awhile. I think she told them to treat her replacement with respect, something like that. She believed in her kids, loved them."

Terry Robinson, a former student who became a special education teacher and taught with Mary for a number of years, said, "Mary taught me how to be strong emotionally." She talked about their Depression glass expeditions, and attending Mass together in Mary's last year. "Her faith never failed her, she never questioned it," she said, "and when I asked her about her illness, she said, 'And why not me?'"

Terry Robinson related a story about Mary's last weekend: It seems that Mary was the only teacher in her school who made her students sing "My Country 'tis of Thee" after the Pledge of Allegiance. The weekend she died, she asked her visitors to sing it for her one more time, saying, "Hit it, girls!" Her caregivers sang, not very well, for Mary said, "I don't think I'll ask you to do that again."

Several hundred people attended the funeral Mass at St. Joseph the Worker. There would have been many more, but the schools were in the midst of a February break. During the service, the priest place two objects on the casket: a gold cross representing Mary's deep faith, and a single rose, emblematic of the love that Mary had for her family, her students, and her community.

The priest read from St. Paul's Letter to the Corinthians: "Love suffers long, and is kind...love envies not, nor does it puff itself up...for now abides faith, hope, and love, and the greatest of these is love." On that day, in that church, the love for Mary was palpable, as strong as the love that Mary herself gave to her family, her students, and her community. In his eulogy, the priest said, "Mary wanted children to know that they were loved."

Later, John Conquest, a friend of the family and fellow educator, read the lines he had written in her honor:

"What a friend we have in Mary, wonderful wife,
Mother, and Grandma, she was always there.
What a privilege to know her, but with
God we must share.
What a life, what a beautiful lady,
Always carrying on with a smile,
Even through her pain and suffering,
She would say, 'Sit, don't leave, stay awhile.'
Sometimes Mary would go unnoticed, quietly
Walking through the hall, but the people
Who were around her knew that she cared
About us all.
She was special to her students, and on her
They did depend.
What a warrior, what a fighter,
Until the very end!"

Peter Paige: Big Man with a Big Heart

The flags flew at halfmast last week over the Bellport Fire House, the Yacht Club, Brookhaven Memorial Hospital, and Brookhaven National Laboratory, as the village and the larger community mourned the passing of Peter Paige.

He was a big man with a big heart, generous and compassionate, and if Bellport had royalty, he would have been its benign monarch, ruling from the back deck of the "Ollie," his Consolidate Motors cabin cruiser.

Peter Paige died at Meadowedge, his home in Bellport, on Friday, July 21, two days after his 83rd birthday.

Paige was born in Bellport in 1917 to Douglas Warner Paige and Julia Edey Paige. After graduating from the Choate School, he attended Princeton University. He worked as a photographer for several years in Florida, then joined American Airlines. When World War II began, he served with the U.S. Army Air Corps Transport Command. Stationed in India, he and his crew flew "over the hump," otherwise known as the Himalayas, a number of times.

After the war, Paige became one of the first employees at Brookhaven National Laboratory, where he soon became the Director of Personnel. He retired from the Lab in 1981.

Peter Paige served as a board member at Brookhaven Memorial Hospital in East Patchogue for 30 years. He served as chairman of the board from 1984 until 1988, and for two more years as interim chairman. He was one of the earliest proponents of the hospital's hospice program, which, as fate would have it, helped his family care for him during his last days at home.

A life-long sailor, Paige was known and respected the length and breadth of Great South Bay, achieving great success in the Star Class sailboat, where he won regional and national trophies. He served for four years as commodore of the Bellport Bay Yacht Club, which celebrated him as a "sportsman, raconteur, dog lover, genial host, regatta committee member, skipper par excellence, cruising buff, and all-around bon vivant," when he was awarded the Paul S. Bigelow Award in 1967.

He was a Chief and life member of the Bellport Fire Department, having joined that organization at the age of 16. He was also captain of the department's first engine company.

In his later years, Paige found pleasure in reading, including books by John Grisham and Tom Wolfe. Often, according to his wife Natalie, he would write critiques on the inside covers of paperbacks, saying, "Don't waste your time on this one!" He and his wife also enjoyed traveling, especially on the Lindblad Expeditions, and working in the garden of the United Methodist Church, where they were members.

Peter Paige is survived by Natalie Lambing Paige, his bride of 56 years; three sons, Peter Otis Paige of Yardley, Pennsylvania, Douglas Warner Paige of Robbinsville, New Jersey, and Lee Allen Paige of North Andover, Massachusetts; two sisters, Mary Paige McGuirk of Bel Air, Maryland,

and Sheila Paige Dominy of Shelter Island; and seven grandchildren.

At his request, Paige's body was donated to the Stony Brook University Medical School for research.

Pehaps Peter Paige's life is best summed up by some lines penned by his grandmother, Birdsall Otis Edey, suffragette, writer, and national leader of the Girl Scouts. In a poem called "A Grandmother's Prayer," she wrote of her grandson and his friends:

"Teach them the truth, give them the strength to say,
Thy will be done and mean it, every day.
And that one who is mine, teach him to see
The right, to face his life without fear, to be
Considerate, and then, take care of him for me."

She got her wish.

Nancy Ljungqvist: A lover of Bellport

When Nancy Tibbs Ljungqvist was honored by the village of Bellport in 1996 for over 30 years of service, she declined to speak at the awards ceremony. That was her way.

Despite her quiet, self-effacing manner, Nancy Ljunagqvist was active as a local merchant, landlord, member of the Chamber of Commerce, the Bellport-Brookhaven Historical Society, the Bellport Bay Yacht Club, and the Playcrafters, a local dramatic society.

Typically, she also wanted to share the honor with the village itself. Instead of having her picture taken, she said, "The picture should be of all of us, not just me. It should be a picture of everyone in Bellport, where we are all held together by a common thread. No matter who we are, what we do, or where we came from, we all love Bellport."

"Nancy is an old-timer who will be sorely missed," said Bellport Mayor Frank C. Trotta. "She was a straight shooter who clearly loved the village, and always a giver."

For these reasons and many others, local residents were saddened to hear that Nancy Ljungqvist died at the age of 77 after a short illness. She is survived by her husband Ed, two sons, Peter and Bruce, and four grandchildren.

Born in New York City, Nancy Ljungqvist went to school in Dobbs Ferry, wintered in Florida, and spent her summers in Bellport. She attended Finch Junior College, and then decided to go to work at Georg Jensen, a firm specializing in silverware and Copenhagen china. She also worked for a time with a textile company and Yachting Magazine.

She met her husband Ed while sailing the waters of Great South Bay. Before the birth of their children, the Ljungqvists were active members of the yacht club. In a 1966 interview with the Advance, she said, "I started racing at age 13 in a Cape Cod One design. Later, we moved up to a Narrasketuck. When the children came along, we bought our house and sold the boat."

Nancy opened a small gift shop on Bellport's Main Street in 1946, staying open from the summer until Christmas and paying $5.00 a month rent. "We had to close after Christmas because we had no heat, but I made a profit every month," she said.

Once her sons were off to school, Nancy decided that being a charter member of the Playcrafters and the historical society was not enough, so she started a children's clothing shop called The Outrigger, in the space which was the original site of an ice cream parlor, one of her favorite childhood haunts. She opened a second shop called the Penguin's Pantry a few years later.

The Ljungqvists joined the Playcrafters and worked backstage for the group's first performance, "Bell, Book, and Candle." "We took our children along, and they played on a blanket during rehearsals," she said.

Nancy also became a board member of the Bellport-Brookhaven Historical Society. She had a particular interest in this organization, as one side of her family, the Smiths, have lived in the area since 1685.

Nancy was not only interested in the past. She believed that Bellport had a future. "More and more, people want to come to a village where they know who they're talking to, where the chamber of commerce stresses volunteerism and working for the good of the village," she said. "Bellport is a village that makes you want to do for it."

After she was honored by the village in 1996, Nancy said she had one piece of unfinished business: parking in the village. She said, "When my time comes to go to that pretty piece of green on the west side of Station Road (the cemetery), instead of the traditonal grave marker, I would like to borrow a sign from the village that reads 'Two Hour Parking Strictly Enforced.'"

It is also characteristic of Nancy Ljungqvist that instead of a funeral service, she wanted to invite family and friends to a party later in the spring, when the Isotope Stompers could play "When the Saints Come Marching In."

When that happens, we can be sure that Nancy will be there, enjoying the occasion.

Gino Robbiano: Chef, Resterateur

During its halcyon years, the Better Ole Restaurant was a favorite watering hole for the rich and famous, as well as local residents. During the filming of "Splendour In the Grass" on the grounds of the nearby Tiger Nursery in Brookhaven, Warren Beatty, Natalie Wood, and director Elia Kazan dined there, along with many other Hollywood and Broadway notables.

They enjoyed food prepared by chefs and propietors Gino and Joseph Robbiano.

The hamlet of Brookhaven was saddened to learn of the death of Gino M. Robbiano, age 77, at Brookhaven Memorial Hospital.

Born in Salt Lake City, Utah, Robbiano has been a local resident since 1941. He served in the U.S. Army Air Corps in World War II, and became a member of the local Masons.

Gino Robbiano is survived by hs wife Christine, daughters Gina Varney of Patchogue and Carla Liuzzi of Albany; two grandchildren, Brian and Michael Varney; two brothers, Joseph Robbiano of Brookhaven and James Robbiano of Florida, and his niece, Daria Dolan, a radio and television financial advisor, who lives in Greenwich, Connecticut.

Elinor Hughes Jacobus

On Sunday, March 15, friends and family members made their way to the Academy House in Bellport to celebrate the life of Elinor Hughes Jacobus, who died on February 28, three days short of her ninety-second birthday, and her husband David D. Jacobus, who predeceased her by more than ten years.

Mr. and Mrs. Jacobus first came to Bellport when he took a position as an engineer at Brookhaven National Laboratory.

A former drama critic for the Boston Herald, Mrs. Jacobus became actively involved with the Fireplace Literary Club, writing up publicity notices and giving talks about her wide-ranging interests. She knew what she was talking about, for Ms. Jacobus had been the drama critic of the Boston Herald for over 40 years, writing about and meeting the likes of Moss Hart and George S. Kaufman. She wrote for the Herald at a time when many shows were previewed by audiences in Boston and New Haven before they took their chances on the Great White Way in New York.

Writing under the name of Elinor Hughes, she started working for the newspaper right after her graduation from Radcliffe, and her reviews, which occasionally included film and music, made her a leading voice in Boston as she covered hundreds of Broadway-bound musicals and dramas. Her encyclopedic knowledge of English and American prose and poetry, especially Shakespeare, from which she could quote liberally, made her writing interesting and erudite. According to her friends, Hamlet was her favorite Shakespearean play, and she knew it by heart. Many of her reviews were collected in her book, Passing Through To Broadway. She also authored two anthologies about famous stars of filmdom. Moreover, she had the distinction of playing herself in a film, "Teacher's Pet," which starred Rock Hudson and Doris Day.

Of her work, she said, "I was fortunate in many respects, knowing from the age of 13 years what I wanted to do, parents who provided me with a first-rate education, and a home where I could live before I was sufficiently established to support myself; having friends who opened doors for me that I could not have opened myself; and employers who, if a bit doubtful that a 27-year-old woman could head the drama department of a metropolitan newspaper, gave me the opportunity and later confirmed me."

Ms. Jacobus became the doyenne of a group known as "the Boston Girls," critics and journalists who were breaking into what was previously a male-dominated field.

At the age of 51, she married David D. Jacobus, whose wife had died an untimely death. With the marriage, there came two stepsons, David P. Jacobus of Princeton, who would add five grandchildren and four great-grandchildren to the clan, and John Henry Jacobus, who lives in New York.

Her new life in Bellport was filled with gardening, the local literary scene, and trips to the opera and theater in New York City. Her stepdaughter-in-law, Claire Jacobus, said, "It was such a pleasure to go to the theater with her. She brought a sense of excitement. She was so knowledgeable, yet attentive to what others thought. She took great pleasure in introducing her children and grandchildren to the theater, especially if it was a revival of a play she had reviewed up in Boston, like The King and I."

According to Mary Alburger, an old friend, "She belonged to the Opera Guild, had seats in the front row, you know. When she went to the opera, they stayed at the Algonquin." Ms. Alburger also reminisced about Fireplace Literary Club Christmas parties held at the Academy house, where Mrs.

Jacobus would reign, wearing her traditional black velvet hostess gown with a multicolored sash, and black velvet slippers.

Another friend, Ann Potter, remembered Ms. Jacobus in her later years, no longer gardening, but sitting in the corner of a favorite sofa with her reading glasses, books, television remote, watching baseball, basketball, or hockey. Potter said, "She loved to watch sports on television." Woody Allen once said that there was a strong connection between sports and theater, with the elements of protagonist versus antagonist, struggle, and outcome, so it is not surprising that the drama critic would spend her final years enjoying sports on television.

So as her friends and family gathered on Sunday to listen to a reading of one of her reviews set in verse, as well as the music from her extensive collection of records, they celebrated the life of an extraordinary woman, a woman who could recite baseball statistics and Shakespearean verse with equal ease, a woman for all seasons, Elinor Hughes Jacobus.

Phyllis Shreeve

Our town was saddened last week to hear of the passing of Phyllis Heidenreich Shreeve, 78, on Friday, June 9, 2000.

Ms. Shreeve cared deeply about environmental issues, and was active in the Carmans River Coalition, established to protect that waterway. She was also an accomplished weaver and a member of the Potters' Club.

An avid reader and a member of a book club, she shared her love of the printed word by volunteering as a reading teacher in the public schools. She also worked as a physician's assistant for the late Dr. Edith Forsyth.

Her daughter Elizabeth said, "Hers was the house where all our teenage friends went to talk, to drink tea, to play music." Ms. Shreeve played the piano, the recorder, and sang, and passed her love of music on to her three children.

"She had that Hoosier charm, she could make friends with a dream pipe, and loved to meet young people," her daughter said.

Phyllis Shreeve was born in Indianapolis, Indiana. In high school, she was the co-editor of the school newspaper, along with novelist-to-be Kurt Vonnegut. She graduated from Dennison University, Ohio, in 1944, and earned her Master's degree in bacteriology at Indiana in 1945. For a time, she worked at Brookhaven National Laboratory.

Phyllis Shreeve is survived by her husband, Dr. Walton Shreeve; three sons, Thomas of Arlington, Virginia, Daniel of Iron Mountain, Michigan, and James of Silver Springs, Maryland; a daughter, Elizabeth Robinson, of Mill Valley, California; and eight grandchildren.

A memorial gathering was held at the Post Morrow House in Brookhaven on June 14. The family requested that in lieu of flowers, donations should be made to the Post Morrow Foundation or the Environmental Defense Fund.

In the memorial program, there appeared lines penned by Phyllis Shreeve when she was a high school student, words that seem to provide a fitting epitaph to a full and active life:

Where go the years?
But moments fleet, uncertain
That swiftly speed and disappear
From mortal view?
Where go the years?
To seek the darkness and to hide
Within the dust of old hall clocks?
Or ride forgotten moonbeams to the sky?

Walter P. Geoghan

Walter P. Geoghan, a longtime Bayport resident and the founder of the insurance agency bearing his name, died Saturday of brain cancer at Good Samaritan Hospital in West Islip. He was 71.

Walter Geoghan was born in Brooklyn on March 28, 1925. He graduated from Brooklyn Prep in 1943, and served in the U.S. Army in Germany during World War II.

After the war, he attended St. John's University, where he played basketball and majored in business administration, graduating in 1951.

He worked for a financial institution in the 1950s, and in 1957 he established his insurance agency, where he worked until his retirement in 1994.

Mary Murphy, one of the staff members there, said, "He had many employees who had been there for 20 to 30 years. He was fun, a pleasure to work with."

Walter Geoghan was a founding member and the first president of the Bayport-Blue Point Chamber of Commerce. He was the grand marshal of the first Bayport-Blue Point St. Patrick's Day Parade.

He was also active in the Suffolk County Independent Insurance Agents Association and served several terms as its treasurer.

An avid sportsman, Walter Geoghan loved golf, swimming, and sailing. He played a major role in the reactivation of the Sayville Yacht Club in the early 1950s and later served as its commodore. He and his wife Gail loved to travel and recently returned from a trip to the Far East.

In addition to his wife, survivors include his sister, Gloria McGuirk of Stuart, Florida; his brother, Jack Geoghan, of Westhampton; his daughter, Kathleen Geoghan Remmer; sons Peter, Michael, Christopher, John, Walter Pierce, William Pierz, and Matther Pierz; and 14 grandchildren. He was predeceased by his youngest son, Brian.

Bernie Lyons

According to Ken Russell, his boss at Reese's 1900, Bernie Lyons's conversations never started with the usual "hello." They always began with the words, "Hey, did you hear the one about…"

The owner of what is considered by many as a local version of "Cheers" credits Lyons for the friendly ambience of the place. "Bernie made it that way," said Russell, speaking of the convivial atmosphere established by Lyons during his seven years as bartender and chief raconteur.

Bernie Lyons, born in the Bronx but a resident of Patchogue for most of his life, died on December 18, 1996, at the age of 32, after a long illness.

Russell said, "He was a class individual, and a very competitive, tenacious guy, whether playing tennis or shuffleboard. His tenacity came out when he was dealing with his illness, too, and he lived longer than the doctors expected. We will miss his stories and the laughs, but we take comfort knowing our loss is heaven's gain."

Russell added, "We had a customer from Rochester, a traveling salesman, came in once a year, but Bernie always remembered him, saying, 'Hi, Rochester.' The guy always answered, 'Bernie, this place looks like a Norman Rockwell painting.' Bernie was like that, he could animate a still-life painting, bring it to life with his personality. He was an artist without a brush."

Bernie Lyons is survived by his wife Lori; his parents Bernard and Carolyn; three sisters: Doreen Hummel, Karen Lyons, and Kathleen Lyons; and two brothers, Kenny and Tommy. Most of the family resides in Melbourne, Florida.

According to friends, Lyons will be particularly missed by his best friend Mandy, a cocker spaniel.

Clovis Campbell

The hundreds of runners who crossed the finish line each year at the Clipper Classic road race in Bellport probably did not know Clovis M. Campbell, but they were grateful for the cup of water she handed them.

This image seems to sum up the life of Clovis Campbell, a quiet, unassuming, special education teacher who died on Saturday, January 26, at University Hospital in Stony Brook. She was 55.

At the time of her death, Clovis Campbell was surrounded by her family, including her daughter Kimberley, who was at the time attending Clemson University and has since married, become a mother of two and a physician's assistant.

On the walls of the hospital room there were dozens of get well cards created by Ms. Campbell's students, a silent testimonial to the impact she had on youngsters at the Frank P. Long Intermediate School for 32 years. The cards are also a reflection of her interest in painting, especially watercolors and animals; she was an active member of the South Bay Art Association.

Growing up in Sag Harbor, Ms. Campbell earned her bachelor's degree at Southampton College and went on to get her master's degree at Hofstra University.

She is predeceased by her father Sam King, and survived by her mother, Evelyn King; her daughter Kimberley; sisters Dorothy Kessen of East Hampton and Lenis Hearn of Sandusky, Michigan; and six nephews and nieces.

After a well-attended wake at the Yardley and Pino Funeral Home, the interment took place at the family plot in Oakland Cemetery in Sag Harbor. The family has requested that memorial donations be made to the American Cancer Society.

On Clovis Campbell's burial stone reads the inscription: "Mother, teacher, artist: beloved by all who knew her."

A fitting epitaph for a woman who devoted her life to the service of others.

Farewell to a Firehouse Legend:
John Masem, Sr.

Almost every fire department on Long Island has a spiritual leader, a legend in his own time. Such a man was John A. Masem, Sr. who died on March 10 at the age of 72.

Last week, John Masem lay in state at the new firehouse in Medford that was dedicated in his honor several months previously, as members of the fire service from all over Long Island lined up to pay homage. Also in attendance were teachers and former students from the Longwood School District, where Masem had been a respected educator, coach, and guidance director, shaping the lives of thousands of students over the years.

A graduate of St. Bonaventure University, John Masem served with the U.S. Air Force as an observer during the Korean War. He was also a lector at St. Sylvester's R. C. Church in Medford. He was a member of the Medford Fire Department for more than 40 years, serving as chief and commissioner.

Active in many state, county, and local firematic organizations, Masem was a past president of the Suffolk County Firefighters Association, secretary of the Brookhaven Town Volunteer Firefighters Association, secretary of the

Vocational Board of the Fire Academy in Yaphank, board member of the Southern New York Volunteer Firefighters Association, and a member of the Firefighters Association of the State of New York. For many years, he was a trustee of the New York State Fireman's Retirement Home.

John Masem Sr. is survived by his wife Mary; two sons, John Jr. and David; two daughters, Kathleen Zguris and Nancy Sargent; and a sister, Jane Olafsen; and seven grandchildren.

John Masem Sr. has passed on a living legacy in the Medford Fire Department: his son, John Jr. is serving as member and ex-chief; his grandson, John III, is a captain of the Junior Firefighters; and his granddaughter, Jennifer, has joined the ranks of the "probies."

"He was very proud ot them," said his son, John Jr.

On the day of his funeral, John Masem Sr. was placed on an antique fire truck and accompanied by his son and grandchildren to a funeral mass at St. Sylvester's R. C. Church, followed by interment in Holy Sepulcher Cemetery in Coram.

On John Masem's prayer card there are two images: a rendering of Saint Florian, the patron saint of firefighters, and the smiling countenance of John Masem himself, as he will be remembered by the community and the many students whose life he affected. In his own quiet way, John A. Masem Sr. was a saint, too.

Lou Grasso

Lou Grasso was the journalist's journalist. Whether editing weekly newspapers from Center Moriches to Smithtown, or leading the fight against the Shoreham nuclear facility, Lou Grasso was loved and respected by just about everybody in the newspaper business.

Grasso, who only last year successfully battled cancer in his leg, died last week of a massive heart attack in his Medford home. He was 70. Grasso had just returned from a day of fluke fishing on the "Glory Too" and was celebrating the 38th anniversary of his first date with his wife Suzanne.

Grasso was the man who had covered the Suffolk County beat for more than 30 years, editing papers like the Suffolk Life, the Riverhead News Review, the Smithtown Messenger, the Suffolk County News, and the Moriches Bay section of the Long Island Advance.

He was also the man who saw the rise and fall of local polliticos like Zeidler and McNamara, the man who fought for Bayview General Hospital and against the Shoreham nuclear plant, the man who worked with the legends of local journalism lore: Captain John Tuthill, Don Moog, Karl Grossman, Don Meyers, and David Wilmott.

Grasso spent the last 16 years of his career with the Suffolk Life, a free publication mailed to about 500,000 homes throughout Suffolk County. He retired three years ago to pursue his passions: fishing, golf, and golden retrievers. He and his wife bought a home in Orlando, Florida, where they planned to move permanently next year.

Grasso was known for his hard questions. State Assemblyman Paul Harenberg (D-Oakdale) said, "Being interviewed by Lou was an odd combination of being gently wrestled to the mat with flair and finesse by a kindly gentleman...on rare occasions, was enjoyable; it was often humorous; it was never forgettable."

Grasso got his start in the newspaper business as a circulation manager for the Long Island Press. From there he went on to become the circulation director of the Suffolk Consolidated Press, a consortium of weeklies including such papers as The Islip Bulletin, The Smithtown Star, and The Babylon Eagle.

In an interview with The Advance almost three years ago, Grasso said, "I cut my editor's teeth at The Long Island Advance, covering the Moriches Bay section. Back in those days, it was the Moriches Tribune and The Patchogue Advance. The Captain hired me, and he was the fairest guy in the world. They did a study, and decided to combine the two papers, to become The Long Island Advance."

His mentor was Don Moog, who, in an ironic turnabout, worked for Grasso on the Suffolk Life copy desk for eight years after his retirement from the Advance.

Grasso said his proudest moment at the Advance was when he won the Community Service Award from the New York State Press Association for his fight to save Bayview General Hospital in Mastic.

Later in the interview, Grasso said, "I didn't want to leave The Advance, but I wanted the challenge of being an editor." He took over the helm of the Suffolk County News in Sayville, where, he said, "The people had great heart, and the newspaper brought it out." His peak experience there was when he ran a youngster's letter, clled "Freddy's Christmas Wish," requesting a kidney dialysis machine for his father. Grasso said, "We got checks from New York and New Jersey. The machine cost $8,000. We gave Freddy and his mom a check for "$12,000."

While in Sayville, Grasso became the president of the local Rotary, which used to sponsor outings at the beach for the Fresh Air Fund and handicapped children from a Brentwood School. This led to a Grasso column called "The Impossible Dream," which evolved into a project that sent 20 wheelchair-bound children and their chaperones to Disney World.

Grasso said, "In Sayville, all you had to do was write a story, and people would call up to help."

"A newspaper has to have a heart," he added.

While running the Suffolk County News, Grasso won another Community Service Award for his efforts to protect the environmental sanctity of what is now Connetquot State Park, a limited-access refuge for wildlife.

Grasso said the biggest story he covered at Suffolk Life was the fight against the Shoreham nuclear facility. "I think we had a big impact," he said. "We brought the public's attention to the problems they were having. The paper was the last resort for people who were battling the bureaucracy."

Even after retirement from Suffolk Life, Grasso continued to write for the paper on matters of energy and politics.

In addition to his wife, Grasso is survived by his brother, Martin Grasso of Steinhatchee, Florida, and his sister, Marge Marrinen of Queens.

A wake was held at the Ruland Funeral Home in Patchogue, followed by memorial services at the Emanuel Lutheran Church.

The family has requested that in lieu of flowers, contributions may be sent to the Kent Animal Shelter in Calverton, Breast Cancer Help in West Islip, or the Emanuel Lutheran Church in Patchogue.

Prominent among the memorabilia at the wake was "The Angler's Prayer":

God grant that I may fish
Until my dying day,
And when at last I've come to rest,
I'll then most humbly pray;
When in His landing net I'm safely asleep
That in His mercy I'll be judged
As good enough to keep.

Considering the life and times of newspaperman Lou Grasso, we may safely assume that he was "a keeper."

****

Mr. Chuck Anderson
Long Island Advance
Patchogue, New York

Dear Mr. Anderson,

It has taken me too long to thank you for the beautiful article you wrote about my husband, Lou. His tragic sudden death, in July, has left me devastated.

You touched on many facets of his life, his sense of fairness, the importance of community, and his influence on others. He was a teacher and a father figure to his many young reporters, but he truly had no concept of the impact he had on people. He did what he thought he was supposed to do as a good human being.

Lou had a gentle soul. He loved life--birds, flowers, his family--and all that we shared. My life is incredibly meaningless without him.

Copies of your sensitive, insightful article have been sent to family and friends around the country: Florida, Texas, Arizona, Virginia, the Carolinas, and others. Each time someone reads it, they cry.

Lou's giving has not ended. His corneas were donated to the Eye Bank so that two others might regain their sight. I have also been notified that individuals have launched a scholarship program at Suffolk Community College in Lou's memory. Dave Wilmott at Suffolk Life would have more details.

The Suffolk County Legislature has also passed a resolution naming the lobby at the County Center in Riverhead, "The Lou Grasso Lobby." I don't know when the dedication will be, but how fitting, for the lobby is the "people's place."

Thank you for giving me a wonderful article about Lou to treasure and share with others. He would have liked it.

Very sincerely,

Suzee Grasso

George Usher

Recently we talked with George Usher, sportswriter, about his retirement from Newsday and his plans for the future. There was conversation about immediate plans, of spending the summer at his Blue Point beach house with his grandchildren and the usual mob of guests, family, and friends. There were brief words about his new job at St. Joseph's College, as sports information director. Alas, all this was not to be.

George Usher, 68, died Saturday night at his beloved beach house, quietly, in his sleep. Usher's childhood friend, Tom "Red" Murphy, with whom he played ball on the playground at St. Francis de Sales and later on the fields and basketball court of Seton Hall High School, telephoned us with the news. Murphy and Usher had something else in common besides a lifelong friendship: they are both members of the Suffolk County Sports Hall of Fame. Murphy said of his friend, "If everybody who owed George money came to the wake, his family would be set for life."

But this eulogy is not about George Usher's years of fame and fortune during his 25 years at Newsday, the glory years of covering the Jets and the Mets, the NASCAR 500 and the U.S. Open, his legacy of pages and pages of graceful prose.

This is a story about the man, and how he lived. It's about a boy who grew up on the poor side of Patchogue, folding newspapers in the stationery store to help his family. It's about the boy who surprised his friend Tom one day by announcing that he was going to St. John's University. It's about the young man whose education was interrupted by a tour of duty with the Navy during the Korean War, then returned to finish his education at Adelphi-Dowling.

As Murphy says, George Usher lived life to the fullest. He had friends all over the world, yet found the time for Joe Gardi, a former Jets coach, getting him a job with Hofstra University.

Then there is his family: his wife, Dawn, cared for in a Smithtown nursing home, whom he visited on a weekly basis for the past nine years; his sons, Kevin Usher of East Patchogue and Lawrence Usher of Manorville; a daughter, Darlene Usher of Bayport; an adopted daughter, Christine Troche of Patchogue; and his younger brother, Richard Usher. There are also four grandchildren, of whom he was inordinately proud.

Perhaps the best measure of the man is to look at the book he kept for guests at the beach house, a log for people to write in after they had enjoyed a traditional Long Island garbage pail clambake or a meal of pasta with special Usher clam sauce.

Some notes from the beach house diary:

"So I've done some dumb things. The dumbest was when I caught about 20 crabs and put them in a broken basket. The bottom fell out, and the crabs fell into the bay around my feet. I jumped so much that I scared about 19 crabs away."-George

"This is my friend."-Joe Namath

"Two guys were running down the beach. I asked them where they were going. They said, 'George is trying to find a gas leak with his lighter.'"-Bob Rigone

"Look, it's not so bad being a dog in this family."-Morgan, Darlene's yellow Labrador retriever, who was George's constant companion until a fatal bus accident a month ago.

"Let us tell you about our father. He is interesting and loving, a people person, the most caring person we know. He loves to share his beach house with everyone, wants people to enjoy this beach the way he does."-Kevin and Darlene

This week, the family and friends of George Usher traveled to Robertaccio's Funeral Home in Patchogue to pay their respects in a shrine of photographs, flowers, and mementos. The service was followed by interment at Washington Memorial Park in Coram.

We heard that when they brought George Usher home on Sunday morning, they drove him down the early morning beach in a Blazer, then transported him back to Patchogue on the ferry, a solitary passenger, crossing the bay, waves sparkling in the bright sunlight. George would have liked that.

Somewhere there is another beach, in a place where sportswriters go when their game is over. We are sure to find Geoge Usher there, with his dog Morgan frisking at his side. Rest in peace, old friend.

Epitaph for a Sailor: Skip Etchells

Local sailors were saddened to hear of the death of E. W. "Skip" Etchells on December 20, 1998, at his home on the eastern shore of Maryland.

While Skip and his wife Mary never lived on the Great South Bay, many local residents who sailed in the majestic Star Class boats, or were part of the bay's great sailing fleet of the 1940s and 1950s, remember the Etchells well.

Near the end of World War II, Skip and Mary came from Southern California, where he had been building destroyers for the Navy, to settle in Old Greenwich, Connecticut. A naval architect by training, Skip brought a Star Class boat he had built to his own design.

He brought the specially-designed boat to Long Island Sound, the birthplace of the Star, to test his ideas and establish a Star Boat building business.

His boat, named the Shllalah, was first seen on the Great South Bay in August, 1944, when the Atlantic Coast championships were held off Bellport. At the end of the first race, the Shillalah crossed the finish line ahead of the competition.

That was only the beginning.

In the next four races of this memorable series, no boat crossed the Shillalah's bow. It was unheard of in those days to see a woman as crew of a Star boat, but Skip and Mary ended the week's racing with five first places to become the Atlantic Coast champions. From that day on, all other Star boats were judged to be obsolete, and orders for Skip's design began pouring in.

Skip and Mary went on to win many other races: the Atlantic Coast Championship in 1944, 1945, and 1947, and the mid-winter championship in Havana, Cuba, in 1950.

Skip built a new boat for himself, named Shannon, and in 1951, Skip and Mary, sailing that boat, became world champions on the Chesapeake Bay. The duo defeated 48 other fleet champions from all over the world.

In 1953, Skip and Mary came back to the Great South Bay, this time with the Shannon, and raced in the William H. Picken Jr. Memorial Series, which consisted of three races off Bellport. There were 43 boats in this event, probably the pinnacle of Star Boat Racing in the Great South Bay.

When the last boat crossed the finish line, Skip and Mary had placed second, first, and first in the three races, almost another clean sweep.

Great South Bay has had many superb sailors since the days of the great Star races, but few will be as memorable as Skip and Mary Etchells.

Dennis Puleston

On Father's Day we met with the surviving offspring of Dennis Puleston to talk about the extraordinary life of their father, a naturalist, boat designer, ornithologist, adventurer, and founding chairman of the Environmental Defense Fund, which played a leading role in getting insecticide DDT banned in the United States.

His daughter, Jennifer Clement, said, "He used to row us out to John Bayles Island to get his back in shape after being injured in the war. He would tell us fanciful stories about a magical ship that was so big it wouldn't fit in the English Channel. The ship had a hull made of straw, and when it traveled to the South Pacific, the sea horses ate it and it sank. Of course, the surviving crew members never grew old."

Another daughter, Sally McIntosh, said, "He would go for an hour's walk every morning before going off to work at Brookhaven National Lab. He took the family dog and an old pair of binoculars that didn't work very well."

His son Pete said, "I remember he would take carloads of kids out to Montauk Point and Gardiners Island to look at the birds. He never complained about his back, which was broken in six places in the war."

Pete spoke of other field trips with local high school students to Hawk Mountain in Pennsylvania, New Hampshire, Cape May, and Wellington, Florida. "He inspired a lot of these kids to become naturalists, too," he said. Pete added, "For almost four years I was his cabin mate on some Lindblad expeditions to the Antarctic. He never wore a hat or gloves, only a Fair Island sweater his sister had given him."

At the age of 95, Dennis Puleston died on June 8, 2001, at his home in Brookhaven. He was predeceased by his first son, anthropologist Dennis Edward Puleston, who died in 1978, struck by lightning while standing on El Castillo, a pyramid at Chichen Itza in the Yucatan Peninsula. In his book, The Gull's Way, Dennis spoke of his son's passing: "We suffered a deep, irrparable loss. One does never completely recover from a loss of that magnitude."

Dennis Puleston was born in England on December 30, 1905, and grew up in the fishing village of Leigh-on-Sea on the Thames Estuary in Essex. While there, he acquired a love of boats and birds. His uncle introduced him to a lifelong interest in orinthology, and his artist mother encouraged him to draw and paint. He studied biology and naval architecture at the University of London, and after an unsatisfactory period working in a bank, he took his savings and bought a small sailing vessel. In 1931, he left England to begin a six-year sailing adventure around the world, chronicled in his first book Blue Water Vagabond: Six Years Adventure at Sea.

During his odyssey he dined with cannibals in New Guinea, flirted with virgins in Samoa, managed a coconut plantation in the Virgin Island, adopted a pet boa constrictor, tattooed his arm with shark's teeth, searched for sunken treasure off Santo Domingo, was shipwrecked on Cape Hatteras, and taught sailing in Long Island Sound. In 1937, he reached

China just as the Sino-Japanese War was beginning. Almost broke, with little supplies, as they neared the Phillipines, they encountered a Japanese ship collecting specimens for the Emperor's private zoo. Puleston presented the chief officer on the ship with three annoying cockatoos that had been eating his colored pencils, leaving stains all over his sails. Reaching Manila, they were presented with a formidable-looking document acknowledging their gift to the Emperor, along with a newspaper clipping from an English language newspaper. These documents were to prove valuable for Puleston, for as he reached Peking, China, the war was heating up, and the environment became unsafe for westerners. He met a Japanese officer who spoke English and passed him up the chain of command to superiors who were impressed by his connection with the Emperor. Puleston eventually found himself traveling back to Europe on the Trans-Siberian Railway.

Puleston married Betty Wellington in 1939 and became an American citizen in 1942, the year he started working with a firm of naval architects, where he helped design the DUKW, an amphibious landing craft used by the army. Puleston was sent back to the Pacific, where he trained American forces and took part in amphibious operations in the Solomon Islands, New Guinea, and Burma, where he was severely wounded in the spine by a Japanese shell splinter.

After a period in the hospital, Puleston went to Britain to train allied forces in preparation for the Normandy landings. He then went back to the Pacific, organizing a DUKW training school in Oahu and take part in the invasions of Iwo Jima and Okinawa.

After the war, Puleston was appointed Director of Technical Information at Brookhaven National Laboratory. On Long Island, Puleston enjoyed watching the ospreys that arrived every year. In 1948 he visited the Gardiners Island wildlife preserve and found almost 300 nests, with an average of more than two chicks per nest. Returning in succeeding years, he began to find a dramatic fall in the number of active nests.

In 1962 the landmark book Silent Spring by Rachel Carson had been published, revealing the deleterious effects of pesticides on the environment, especially birds. Puleston and other naturalists perceived Carson's findings as "the canary in the coal mine," that pesticides would eventually affect not only birds but other creatures on the food chain. He wrote, "Using DDT to control mosquitos was like torpedoing the Queen Elizabeth II to get rid of rats on board."

Eventually, Puleston and others filed a class action suit against the Suffolk County Mosquito Commission to force the commission to stop the use of DDT. Puleston and his colleagues founded the Environmental Defense Fund in 1967, which has become one of the leading environmental lobbying groups in the United States.

After retiring from Brookhaven Laboratory in 1970, Puleston returned to the sea, beginning a career as a lecturer and guide for the Lindblad organization, accompanying groups of tourists on boat trips all over the world. He went on almost 200 cruises, including about 35 trips to Antarctica.

On his death, the Post-Morrow Foundation in Brookhaven created a trail that led from Beaver Dam Creek down to Great South Bay, called the Dennis Puleston Wildlife Preserve.

At the beginning of Dennis Puleston's book The Gull's Way, there is a quote from John Masefield's "Sea Fever," a fitting epitaph for Dennis:

I must go down to the seas again,
To the vagrant gypsy life,
To the gull's way and the whale's way,
Where the wind's like a whetted knife.

Epitaphs: Having the last word

(In his travels, the author has collected a number of epitaphs. These are some of his favorites.)

"I told you I was sick."- B. P. "Pearl" Roberts, in the Key West Cemetery

"At least we know where he's sleeping tonight."- Key West Cemetery

Also from Key West: "Devoted fan of Julio Iglesias."

"I'm just resting my eyes."-Gloria M. Russell

"God was good to me."

Here lies the body of Jonathan Blake.
Stepped on the gas instead of the brake. -Unionstown, Pa.

Here lies John Yeast. Pardon me for not rising.
Riudoso, N.M.

Here lies Lester Moore
Four slugs from a forty-four.
No Less. No Moore.
-Boothill Cemetery, Tombstone, Arizona

I've finally gotten to the bottom of things.
-Ilka Chase

I'm involved in a plot. -Dorothy Parker

Well, I've played everything but a harp.-Lionel Barrymore

Here lies W.C.Fields;
On the whole, I would rather be living in Philadelphia.

Here lies Walter Winchell in the dirt he loved so much.

Perry Mason: The defense rests.

Good friend, for Jesus' sake forbear
To dig the dust enclosed here

Blessed by the man that spares these stones
And cursed be he that moves my bones.
-William Shakespeare

In Latin:
In vivo fimi sine vivo sum. (I'm up the creek without a paddle.)

Lex clanatoria designati re cindenda este. (The designated hitter has to go.)

Here lies an athiest
All dressed up with no place to go.

I am ready to meet my Maker. Whether my Maker is prepared for the great ordeal of meeting me is another matter.
- Winston Churchill

Would you like to see your manuscript become a book?

If you are interested in becoming a PublishAmerica author, please submit your manuscript for possible publication to us at:

mybook@publishamerica.com

You may also mail in your manuscript to:

**PublishAmerica
PO Box 151
Frederick, MD 21705**

www.publishamerica.com

CPSIA information can be obtained
at www.ICGtesting.com
Printed in the USA
FFOW03n1753070514
5291FF

9 781627 724425